styled

styled

SECRETS FOR ARRANGING ROOMS,
FROM TABLETOPS TO BOOKSHELVES

EMILY HENDERSON

with Angelin Borsics

PHOTOGRAPHS BY DAVID TSAY

POTTER STYLE
NEW YORK

To all my readers and followers. The Internet is a tricky, magical, terrifying, and exciting place that has fostered my relationship with thousands of folks who have helped me grow in every way.

And to my parents, because one should always thank one's parents as publicly and as often as possible.

Photograph on page 151 by Ryan Liebe

Library of Congress Cataloging-in-Publication Data
    Henderson, Emily.
    Styled : secrets for arranging rooms, from tabletops to bookshelves / Emily Henderson. — First Edition.

    1. Interior decoration—Handbooks, manuals, etc. I. Title.
    NK2115.H366 2015
    747—dc23

2014045185

ISBN 978-0-8041-8627-8
eBook ISBN 978-0-8041-8628-5

Printed in China

Book design by La Tricia Watford
Cover design by La Tricia Watford
Cover photography by David Tsay

10

First Edition

contents

introduction

Have you ever wondered why your room doesn't look like the ones in your favorite magazine? No matter how much you decorate, there's still something missing. And it's not fair! You've followed all the rules: You have nice furniture. You've taken a chance on a new wall color you saw on Pinterest. You've even tried arranging your books by color. Then why does everything still feel jumbled, disorganized, and, well, flat?

ENTER THE PROP STYLIST

Here's something you should know: The secret sauce behind those gorgeous rooms in the magazines is the prop stylist, who comes in after everything is set up and tweaks each piece of furniture, accessory, and throw pillow, so that when the camera captures the shot, everything makes sense to the reader's eye.

And here's what that means: You too can have a home that's ready for a magazine shoot, even if Instagram is the actual destination for your pictures. This doesn't take much money, nor does it take a lot of time. And it doesn't require years of art school or an expensive design course on the rules of balance and

scale. All you need are a stylist's secrets, and that's exactly what this book is going to give you.

First, you should know that there are no hard-and-fast rules to styling your home—only *tons* of tricks and tips. Once you try out a few and get the hang of them, everything becomes simpler—shopping becomes less stressful, redecorating becomes fun, entertaining is all of a sudden second nature. *Life* gets easier. Your house will begin to match your personality, and you can finally be that person who exclaims to impressed guests, "Oh, that old thing? I just found it at the flea market and plopped it down right there." Stick with me, and you'll gain the confidence to make anything you touch look amazing.

THIS ISN'T A DECORATING BOOK . . . AND YET IT IS

I started my career as a prop stylist who would run back and forth from a photo shoot to the prop house in order to take rooms from *eh* to *amazing*. Sound exhausting? I loved it. I still love it! When I landed a gig as host of HGTV's *Secrets from a Stylist*, my first step in helping homeowners tailor their rooms to their style was to find out what details they loved (a handbag, a pattern on a pillow). During the process, I realized how styling someone's favorite details in a room is a more accessible approach than trying to decorate it from top to bottom. I mean, who doesn't start with the fun things first, like eating dessert before dinner?

Stylists and interior designers approach rooms very differently. Interior designers are more methodical and often design their clients' homes over a long period of time. They might knock down a wall to open up the kitchen, working closely with an architect to make any structural changes. Dozens of conversations take place before decisions are made so that the client is happy in her new home. We stylists, on the other hand, forgo a drawn-out plan in order to jump right in. We skip the design-professionals-only showrooms and do the shopping ourselves. We follow our noses to unexpected finds at the flea market or beautiful flowers at the farmers' market. You might think we're decorators— except we are more inclined to work with what we've got, obsessing over a room's details and tweaking them in order to bring the room to life.

We might wrap a blanket around a sofa seat rather than reupholstering it, or hang burlap in a window rather than a proper curtain because it matches the rustic vibe we're going for in the room. We'll style natural details like live branches in a vase, books left open, a pair of heels kicked off near a bench, so that it feels like someone actually lives there. "Feels" is key here—stylists care more about how a room feels than what the atmosphere is and if it looks like cool people actually live there. But we also care about how a room functions, especially if it's a space you use every day.

By approaching a room from a stylist's point of view, you free yourself from any anxiety or fear about getting anything wrong. You put on your favorite music and just start playing around—arranging, stacking, and moving things from one surface to another until it all looks right to your eye . . . or until it looks curated in a way you think guests would find interesting. You give yourself time to consider whether you should replace your coffee table. You fell in love with it at some point, right? Maybe a simple refresh is all it needs: replacing the stacks of mail and magazines with a decorative box, a pretty tray, and some art books. You won't really know what works until you can step back and take stock of what you already have.

Then as your vignettes come together and your room takes on a cohesive look, it'll finally feel *decorated*. Don't be surprised if you find yourself opening the door a little wider when neighbors show up at your doorstep. You might even send out the invites for that dinner party you've been putting off— any excuse to get peeps in your place and show it off.

The best way to style your room is to have an idea of what you're going for. And how do you know what you want? You *steal*. Grab ideas from anywhere— magazines, TV, or books, and try them out in your space. Luckily, you've come to the right place.

HOW TO USE THIS BOOK

It probably won't surprise you to hear that styling is one of my favorite things to do, and my biggest goal with this book is to help deconstruct the process for you. Figuring out what style or mix of styles you are is

the foundation to arranging a room where you want to spend all of your time, but that's only the beginning. Then you have to know how to layer all your stuff so that it looks both effortless and yet cohesive.

In The Stylist's Toolkit, you'll take a fun quiz and put a name to your style so you can be more confident when shopping and have an objective for knowing what kind of room you'll like. In Chapter 2, you'll learn the lingo we stylists use on set (including "vignette," "contrast," and "balance") and how those terms apply to styling a room. By then, I know you'll be thinking, *Okay, Emily, when do we actually start getting our hands dirty?*, so Chapter 3 walks you through styling a room from start to finish in ten oh-so-easy steps.

Sound like fun? Well, the second part has even more goodies awaiting you. Room by room, the gorgeous photos and quick takeaways will make your mouth water and get your styling wheels turning. Here I've actually teased out the thinking process behind every vase, folded throw, and patterned pillow. Look for the Photo Tips throughout that give you specific ideas for capturing a vignette or room shot on camera (for instance, knowing the details that'll bring touches of life to your space). Lastly, my Stylist's Notebook compiles insider info on shopping at a flea market, a list of my go-to paint colors, some DIY tips, and all of my favorite resources into one so you can shop just like I do.

My mantra is "Style and play, every day," and I hope you'll start to feel comfortable doing so in your own place. Not only will you end up with a gorgeous home that's the envy of all of your friends, but you'll also have a place that is perfectly suited to your style. (Just don't be surprised if you never want to leave.)

THE STYLIST'S
TOOLKIT

01

NAME YOUR
style

BEFORE YOU CAN STYLE YOUR SPACE, YOU
NEED TO GET TO KNOW WHAT YOU LOVE.

Trying to decorate your house before you understand your style would be like going on a trip to a secluded cabin without any address, directions, or GPS. Sure, you might eventually make it there, but not before some really terrifying things have happened. Most likely you'd just give up.

It took me years to nail down who I am stylistically—and without a guide I wasted so much time and money on unnecessary weird sculptures that cluttered my shelves. I used to walk into my apartment and like everything I saw, but it wasn't until I figured out my own style that my home felt like *me*. Let me save you all of that trouble—it doesn't have to be as painful as my drawn-out process. I am your cautionary tale. You're welcome, America.

WHY NAME YOUR STYLE?

In this chapter, we'll take a moment to put words to your style. You'll find out how to name it, so you can own it. Why does it really matter what style you are? Why take the time to analyze all of your likes and dislikes and figure out if you're Mid-Century or Minimalist? And what, I hear you cry, does all of this have to do with actually styling your space?

REASON 1: Your Home Will Suddenly Feel Super Comfortable

Have you ever noticed how the happiest dogs end up looking like their owners? Well, eventually, your home should resemble you, too. When your home style marries with your personality, there's a certain magic that happens. Your rooms begin to wake up, and you look forward to sinking into your sofa or slipping into bed—not because you're exhausted and can't take any more, but because you can't get enough of the sheer luxury of having your home anticipate your every need. You'll be the most comfortable you've ever been—like, naked-in-seventy-six-degrees comfortable, where you feel no push or pull from your environment.

REASON 2: You'll Become a Pro at Shopping

Let's talk about *things* for a sec. Advertising today is out of control. You might think you have exactly what you want, until you see the next luxe velvet tufted deco sofa, and you think, *How can I live another day without that sofa?!* Then you get it home, and your industrial pipe-frame coffee table, rugged leather ottoman, and seventies shag rug are telling such different stories that instead of looking glamorous and beautiful, you find that your new sofa looks kinda like thrift-store garbage in your place. Wonderful.

At flea markets, you'll eventually find yourself face to face with a diamond in the rough that has the potential to transform your whole living room, or wreck it. Here's the thing: No one else will care about this decision as much as you do—you're the one who has to haggle for it or leave it behind, and when it comes to flea markets (otherwise known as five thousand once-in-a-lifetime opportunities), it can be *very* difficult to pull the trigger or move on. You don't want to mess up and waste money, but you also don't want to regret it later, thinking, *All would be right in my life if only I had bought that huge oil portrait of Tom Selleck from his* Magnum, P.I. *days and hung it over my bed.* Maybe you aren't as dramatic as I am, but retail regrets can lead to temporary depression that only another purchase can heal. It's a terrible and expensive habit.

Once you have a handle on your home style, you won't be riddled with indecision, and shopping will become so much easier. You'll have confidence and tunnel vision when trolling both Craigslist and Crate and Barrel. And when you get that OMG-it's-everything-I-need-in-a-sofa twinge, *you'll know to go with it.* Even when you're a hundred miles from home with no photos of your room in sight. Hello, shopping smarts; good-bye, why-did-I-ever-think-this-thing-would-work feeling. Let's just hope that gorgeous sofa fits.

(You'll learn what your home style is on page 27.)

THINK BEFORE YOU SHOP

While comfort in a home should come first, style is a close second. But don't just fill your home with random stylist props. That'll only make it feel chaotic and, well, random—trust me, I've done it. First, you need to find the basic theme running through your home. Next, ask yourself if you could possibly live without this awesome object you've just found (not just functionally speaking—your room *needs* pretty things). If the answer is absolutely not, then bring it home and give it a place of honor. If the answer is yes, then put it down and move along. Other loves will land in your lap.

REASON 3: You'll Be Able to Edit with Your Eyes Closed

If you're like most people, you may have accumulated a lot of stuff that you don't know what to do with. Some of it has the potential to be perfect props for trying out your new styling techniques—others maybe not so much.

Once you begin styling your space, you'll arrive at the moment when you actually have to pare down those things and decide what should make the cut. How do you know you're not going to regret throwing something out? With your newfound knowledge of your home style, you'll see everything through a more objective lens.

psst . . . look in your closet

One of the easiest ways to pinpoint your home style is to look at what's hanging in your closet. The inspiration for a whole room can come from an outfit that most represents your style. This isn't a foolproof way to decorate—you shouldn't redo your decor as often as you switch fashion styles—but it's a great way to figure out your style inclinations. So in your closet if you spot:

- Mainly taupes, browns, creams, beiges: Don't splurge on a hot pink sofa or paint an accent wall lemon yellow.
- Plenty of vintage pieces: Make time at your favorite flea market to shop the furniture, too.
- A collection of leather jackets and ripped jeans: Stay away from tufted traditional sofas and go for more edgy, "hard-core" pieces.
- Many tailored sheaths, dress shirts, or bow ties (and not just for work): You should probably go for a more "buttoned-up" look at home, too.

- Multiple pairs of the same pants: You like familiarity and comfort. Go for a room with functional ease, like one with a big comfy sofa and a coffee table that you can put your feet on.
- Long, flowy hippie dresses: You should certainly not have a firm, shallow sofa. You are a lounger and you deserve a sofa that suits those needs.

YOU *DO* HAVE A STYLE

Maybe you like a lot of different styles and you don't know where to start. Or *maybe* you feel like you have no style at all. But let me assure you that:

- Any number of different styles can look good together.
- And if you have a personality, you have a style. Even your casualness toward style is considered a style.

We're all a mix of more than one style influence, which makes it hard to know exactly what style or mix of styles our homes should be. If you're still unsure, get an outside perspective: Go shopping with a close friend and ask her to pick out a pair of shoes that flatters your style. Ask her to explain her choice and hone in on the answer. Are the shoes canvas and casual, preppy loafers, or pretty pumps? Ask your friend to choose a second pair and explain. You might just find the confidence you need to move forward.

EMBRACE THE EXPERIMENT

Never regret trying something new or out of your comfort zone. I allow my house to be a style laboratory of sorts; it changes a lot. There are times when a risk turns out to be a total style disaster. For instance, I once painted my guest room two tones of high-gloss green and I liked it for approximately three days before I realized that I actually HATED IT. But many risks have turned out to be big wins. Plus, I always have fun in the end.

NO NEED TO CHOOSE

I've fallen in love with so many different styles, and luckily, I've learned to live with all of them like an extended family. Come over to my house and you'll meet my crazy English grandma (a vintage floral pillow); my mid-century Danish uncle (the leather strapping sofa); my seventies Palm Springs father (a vintage brass collection); my Victorian princess sister (all of my ornate rugs); my Hollywood Regency, chinoiserie-loving mother (my bedroom dresser); my classic early American brother (a simple wood armoire); and my Moroccan bazaar–going stepsister (all my crazy poufs). And that's just my immediate family.

I keep meeting and connecting with new styles and introducing them to each other. At first there's a little bit of tension (jealous, much?), but ultimately they all learn to live together, although not necessarily equally at all times. Much like your average family, some siblings are louder than others, and some cousins don't visit half as much as others do. I might live with ten different styles, but I'm an extreme case, indeed, and I rotate my accessories and decor pretty often. Most people gravitate toward two to three styles, and it's those core styles you need to find, accept, mix, and accentuate.

THE STYLE QUIZ

My first step in working with clients is to find out exactly what style they are. To do so, I always ask them a simple set of questions that's kind of like a game—I call it my style diagnostic, and it really took off on *Secrets from a Stylist*. I'd always start the show by quizzing both homeowners on their favorite accessories or ideal armchair. Then I assigned an uber-specific style name to their personality, like Sexy Afro Glam or Modern Effortless Romance. This process was fun, and it also shaped the whole direction for the episode and gave me the right parameters when shopping for the room.

Finding your home style is not like figuring out whether your car should take premium or regular unleaded. Your style, like your personality, is *very* nuanced and complicated, with lots of conflicting ideas. But because we're so familiar with ourselves, sometimes it helps to get an outside perspective by having someone else tell us what we're into (design therapist, anyone?), which is why I adapted my style diagnostic for this book. It should help you decipher the clues that you give off to the world, but really, it's only the beginning. No one-way quiz (sorry, BuzzFeed fans) will ever get your personality right on the nose.

Here's my style diagnostic dreamed up just for you. Don't let these results box you into just one style; instead, let them be a starting point for discovering all of the cool, interesting things about your personality that you never paid attention to before. And don't just take this quiz once. Take it five or six times. Take it once every six months. Let it help you discover how your style is changing. Once you have your personal mix of styles nailed down, give it a crazy, mishmash name à la *Secrets from a Stylist*, like *Modern Family* Meets *Downton Abbey* Chic to make it yours. Then be sure to Instagram a pic of your new room at #emstylediagnostic.

QUIZ INSTRUCTIONS

- Tell your boss you have food poisoning and need to stay home. Call a sitter for your kids. This is very important to your style future.
- Take this quiz with friends, but only if you all play honestly.
- Grab a notepad, a pen, and a seat in a quiet space.
- Answer the questions, tally your responses, and then find your style match.
- Gush over yourself for a few minutes (no judgments here).
- The grand finale? Flip to page 47 for my style wheel, which works like a color wheel in helping you find your personality counterpart so you can mix and match styles to your heart's desire.

home
style quiz

To start, answer these two questions:

You tend to like furniture with decorative curves, rather than streamlined, straighter styles:
a. Yes
(b.) No

You love to fill your bookshelf with lots of objects, books, and accessories:
a. Yes
(b.) No

If you answered yes to both, skip to questions 11 through 20. If you answered no to either or both, answer questions 1 through 10.

For questions 1 through 10, give yourself 1 point for all the A's you answer, 2 points for all the B's, 3 points for the C's, 4 points for the D's, and so on. Add up your points and jump to pages 32–46 to see your results.

1 **The first thing you do when you get home from work is:**
a. Pour yourself a warm cup of tea and curl up under your hand-knit white throw by the fireplace while you catch up on your favorite street-style bloggers.
b. Hang your Helmut Lang coat neatly in the coat closet, place your keys and sunglasses inside your entry console, and turn up the eclectic jazz music on your Bang Olufsen sound system.
c. Home? You're more likely to peruse the newest art gallery opening before meeting up with friends for a late-night cocktail.
d. Take your shoes off, light a few candles, and wind down by meditating.
e. Put on your house slippers, pour yourself a whiskey on the rocks, and catch up on the latest in the *New York Times.*
f. Hang your vintage bike on your wall hook and continue accessorizing your reclaimed wood bookshelf with your latest flea market finds.

2 **This object caught your eye at the flea market:**
a. A hand-woven wall hanging.
b. An overscale black-and-white graphic print.

c. Lucite stacking boxes.

d. Vintage calligraphy brushes.

e. An iconic Platner stool.

f. Antique radio tubes.

3 **A party at your place might look like this:**

a. Lots of friends and family over to pour back a few glasses of vodka and enjoy an array of desserts before moving on to the newest disco-tech.

b. A few guests to enjoy a sampling of skillfully cooked concoctions by your friend who just opened up a nouveau cuisine restaurant.

c. Some friends enjoying light appetizers while taking in a new art piece that you've been working on.

d. Only the finest fresh sushi skillfully arranged on bamboo platters complete with jasmine green tea shots.

e. A cocktail party with fine liquor, cigars, and plenty of dapper men and women.

f. Opening your loft doors to anyone as long as they bring beer to the party while your DJ friend spins.

4 **Your favorite seat in the house would have to be:**

a. Your wishbone chair that you inherited from your grandmother. Ever since you tossed a fur throw on it, it has become your happy place.

b. Sitting in your sun-soaked dining nook—the morning light hits it just right through the large floor-to-ceiling glass windows and it warms the space just perfectly.

c. Your black Le Corbusier leather chair. You've had it forever and you could never get sick of its sleek lines.

d. Your teak lounger outside in your courtyard— the perfect place to watch the koi as they swim around in the pond.

e. Your Charles Eames lounge chair and ottoman after a long day of work at the office. It's the perfect place to kick off your shoes and enjoy a good book.

f. Your vintage architect's bar stool. Whenever you sit there you can't help but think about all the different people who have loved it throughout the years.

5 **You love shopping here for your home:**

a. Ikea.

b. I already have enough stuff.

c. The nearest modern art museum store.

d. Your favorite Japanese store, Muji.

e. Design Within Reach.

f. The Brooklyn Flea Market.

6 **Which two colors would you want to live with for the rest of your life?**

a. Blue and white.

b. White and black.

c. Slate blue and burgundy.

d. Moss green and taupe.

e. Chartreuse and light peachy-pink.

f. Stone and iron.

7 **The item most likely to sit pretty on your bookshelf is:**

a. A hand-turned blond wood candlestick holder collection.

b. I like to keep my space clean and free of clutter.

c. A hand-blown glass vessel.

d. A vintage brass singing bowl from Tibet.

e. A teak serving tray.

f. Your great-grandfather's typewriter.

8　You'd rather live here:
　　a. Stockholm.
　　b. Tokyo.
　　c. Milan. *(circled)*
　　d. Bali.
　　e. Palm Springs.
　　f. New York City.

9　Your favorite thing to do before you go to bed is to:
　　a. Curl up in front of the fire.
　　b. Read from your tablet.
　　c. Binge-watch the latest Netflix series on your big screen. *(circled)*
　　d. Relax through meditation.
　　e. Smoke a cigar or sip on a little Scotch.
　　f. Tinker with something.

10　Dressing up for you looks a little like:
　　a. A simple A-line dress—with pockets for function, obviously.
　　b. Something structured, classic, and memorable.
　　c. A piece that doesn't call too much attention to itself: fitted, simple, and modest. *(circled)*
　　d. Anything linen—comfortable, organic, soft, and flowy.
　　e. Something iconic and sexy, and maybe adorned with a vintage brooch that says *come on over and chat*.
　　f. You're not one for dressing up, but you always look cool: skinny jeans, a gray T-shirt, and a vintage cognac moto jacket.

If you answered yes to the questions on page 28, start here. Give yourself 7 points for all the A's you answer, 8 points for all the B's, 9 points for the C's, 10 points for the D's, and so on. Tally up your points and flip to pages 32–46 to see your results.

11　Your ideal ride is a:
　　a. Restored 1951 Ford pickup. *(circled)*
　　b. Why ride when you can simply put your thumb out and glide?
　　c. 1970s Volkswagen Bus ready for a road trip.
　　d. Rolls-Royce, outfitted with my own driver.
　　e. DeLorean, especially one that time-travels.
　　f. Jaguar, because it's classic and beautiful.

12　You can't get enough of this textile:
　　a. A natural cowhide rug.
　　b. A worn Turkish kilim. *(circled)*
　　c. An intricately detailed macramé tapestry.
　　d. A luxurious mohair pillow.
　　e. A graphic neon pillow.
　　f. A sumptuous cable knit throw.

13　Your Saturday morning routine looks a little like this:
　　a. A walk around the lakeside. *(circled)*
　　b. A visit to the farmers' market.
　　c. Dancing around in your underwear.
　　d. Sleeping in because you may or may not have had too much to drink last night.
　　e. A good phone chat with a friend.
　　f. Waking up to the sound and smell of sizzling bacon and fried eggs.

14　You would die to live on this movie set:
　　a. Rosalyn Rosenfeld's bold ranchhouse in *American Hustle*.
　　b. The *Grey Gardens* house (before the raccoons got to it).
　　c. Polly's eclectic apartment in *Along Came Polly*.
　　d. Gatsby's home in the original or remake. *(circled)*
　　e. That awesome art deco beach house in *Weekend at Bernie's*.
　　f. Jane Adler's gorgeous house in *It's Complicated*.

15 At the flea market, you're probably eyeing this type of object:

a. An antler set that you can't wait to hang on your wall.

b. A Moroccan wedding blanket—the perfect extra layer for your bed.

c. Retro string art, which looks cool in the right color palette.

d. A silky little number: a hot pink maxi dress from the thirties.

e. A sleek brass table lamp.

f. A linen wingback chair with upholstery in perfect condition. Yeah!

16 The plant most likely to grow in your living room is:

a. A tall potted cactus that looks plucked off a ranch.

b. A sprawling, jungle-like fiddle leaf fig.

c. A resilient, feathery Boston fern.

d. Who has time to water plants?

e. A neon green, trailing ivy plant.

f. A classic spiral-shaped cedar topiary.

17 You're likely to re-cover your favorite armchair in this fabric:

a. A soft off-white or beige linen weave.

b. A bright vintage Indian sari.

c. An oversized poppy floral print.

d. Luxurious velvet damask.

e. Sleek white leather.

f. Something with an Old World vibe, like a chinoiserie print.

18 You could live by this quote:

a. "Ah! There is nothing like staying at home, for real comfort," said Jane Austen.

b. As Allen Ginsberg once advised: "Follow your inner moonlight; don't hide the madness."

c. "I want to rock and roll all night, and party every day," as Gene Simmons would have us do.

d. Marilyn Monroe put it best: "Fear is stupid. So are regrets."

e. Like David Bowie, you believe, "I don't know where I'm going from here, but I promise it won't be boring."

f. "One is born with good taste. It's very hard to acquire. You can acquire the patina of taste," as noted by the one and only Diana Vreeland.

19 You're ready to start a new collection. You start stocking up on:

a. A collection of oil paintings—all landscapes of quiet countrysides.

b. Antique Turkish and Moroccan textiles that remind you of your trip abroad.

c. Vintage wicker and rattan baskets and accessories—you love the natural color and textures they bring to your room.

d. Luxe Lucite accessories or vintage fur—you find them irresistible.

e. Fun brass objects that bring a little bling home.

f. Antique plates and teapots—you're always on the search for more of your grandmother's wedding pattern.

20 Long day at work. You order this at the bar:

a. Nothing fancy—Jack on the rocks should do it.

b. A Mai Tai, or whatever comes with an umbrella so you can pretend you're far, far away.

c. Make it a Harvey Wallbanger (you're always a sucker for a throwback drink).

d. Martini, of course. You know exactly how to order it: extra dry and a little dirty.

e. Oh, why not? Sex on the Beach would be fun to try.

f. Always a glass of their best merlot.

MEET YOUR STYLE
SCANDINAVIAN
(10 TO 19 POINTS)

Hello, Sunshine. You're the nature lover of the minimalist bunch and oh so happy! You celebrate the sun and throw your windows open at every chance to bring in the light. You forgo too many accessories because you want it to feel open and fresh and you're not home much anyway, always enjoying the outdoors while the weather is nice and keeping active during cold months to stave off winter blues.

Scandinavian style celebrates minimalist decor and functional furnishings with a lot of whites, hits of black, wood tones, and a few pops of color to keep things happy and a touch quirky.

LOOK ON THE LIGHT SIDE

- Light woods like maple, birch, and oak
- Plastic modern chairs
- Clean lines
- Natural or whitewashed floors
- Hits of black
- Bright, warm color accents
- Wintry comforts (candles and faux fur)

MINIMALIST

(20 TO 29 POINTS)

Hoarders may think you're uptight and OCD, but you might be the most free of all of your friends. Who needs things? They only get in the way of the life you want to lead. Anything you do bring home involves major consideration. After all, this will *take up space.* So you tend to collect just the attractive versions of the stuff you need, displayed in a simple, organized way.

Minimalist design is stark, clean, and modern—nothing further can be removed to enhance the design, and the spirit of the materials speaks loudly. Great things were born out of minimalism, such as the walls coming down between living rooms and kitchens to create lush, open spaces and furniture that looks like modern art.

LESS IS ALWAYS MORE

- White surfaces
- Chrome accessories
- Streamlined platform beds
- Modern paneled storage
- Spare floating shelves
- Minimal sculptures
- Sleek furniture with simple legs
- Multifunctional pieces

ZEN (30 TO 39 POINTS)

You believe in "flow," and whether you realize it or not, you're always seeking ways to unlock the chi in your rooms: lighting candles or folding your throw so that it lines up perfectly with the sofa. Your home is your haven, so just stick with honest, pure basics.

Zen is an Eastern approach to decorating (or "undecorating") that focuses on the warmth of materials in a minimalist style. These rooms achieve balance, harmony, and relaxation by softening the starkness of minimalism with natural materials, wood accents, and sculptural greenery.

NAMASTE, MY FRIEND

- Tonal or monochromatic color palettes
- Diffused light, such as from paper lanterns
- Essential-oil burners and natural scents
- Solid bedding, rugs, and curtains
- Natural materials, like sustainable woods and linen
- Contrasting textures, like a woven basket on a smooth side table
- Simple furniture with little to no ornamentation
- Indoor plants like terrariums

CONTEMPORARY

(40 TO 49 POINTS)

You have little use for the past. Instead, you live in the here and now and look to the future. But that doesn't mean you're changing your style every five minutes. You know what you like and you stick with it: quiet nights in, clutter-free bookshelves, casual rooms.

My theory is that any current style that doesn't reference the past is Contemporary, but conventionally, this style is sleek and casual, with nothing that feels too over the top. Skip anything too decorative and feminine. But most of all, free yourself of any clutter.

BACK TO BASICS

- Neutral, masculine color palettes
- Color blocking in the accents
- Oversized artwork
- Low, simple sofas
- Glass tables
- Smart, hidden storage (behind walls or in furniture)
- Arc lamps
- Chrome or nickel finishes

INDUSTRIAL (50 TO 59 POINTS)

You're the tinkerer and enjoy a good DIY, a bit unrefined with that whole nerd-cool thing going on, never getting enough of craft beers, built-from-scratch bikes, and record players. You love design in its raw state with its interior still visible so you can figure out how it works. Your dream home would be an abandoned factory loft in Brooklyn with exposed plumbing that matches your shiny Edison lightbulbs hanging from simple plug-in cords. You find yourself collecting lots of metals and woods but never anything too refined or polished.

Industrial style is a more masculine look that has made a huge comeback in the last ten years. Factory carts, typewriter tables, anything that was once utilitarian has become popular furniture in modern homes. Raw and rough surfaces look intentionally unfinished. Old materials are transformed into tables or shelving units. Architectural elements throughout the space stay in view, which can help keep design costs lower.

WHAT'S HAPPENING, HIPSTER?

- DIY pipe shelving
- Chalkboard paint
- Steel kitchen islands
- Subway tile

- Simple pendants with exposed bulbs
- Rusted architectural wall hangings
- Metal chairs

MID-CENTURY MODERN

(60 TO 69 POINTS)

There's nothing extraneous or frilly about your style—everything you wear is impeccable, iconic, and always perfectly put together. You know the power of a slim suit or a simple, elegant shift dress, accessorized with a statement necklace and simple heels. You enjoy dressing up for dinner and might even indulge in a manhattan while cooking (I mean, I do anyway). To you, good design is everything and the death of Steve Jobs was a huge loss. The way he stripped technology down to its most functional state in beautiful, simple designs is total genius. Still reminiscing over that season finale of *Mad Men*? Lucky you; now you can bring the spirit of Don Draper into your home.

Mid-Century Modern is all about masculine, sleek, and sexy shapes with a strong retro vibe. The style emerged in the 1950s and '60s as a rejection of traditionalism's ornamental design and the aristocratic attitude that ruled before World War II. After the war people were optimistic and wanted a change, and so modern furniture and architecture became more democratic with pieces scaled back to their most functional, sculptural, and ergonomic shapes. Furniture became lighter with slimmer legs and more versatile so folks could live simply and rearrange at will. Geometric, bold patterns and neutrals with pops of bright color graced the rooms.

SHAKEN, NOT STIRRED

- Tulip or Eames-style molded plastic chairs
- Warm wood finishes, like rosewood or teak
- Geometric patterns
- Long, streamlined sofas
- Low, long dressers or credenzas
- Bar carts
- Furniture with tapered legs
- Chrome and brass accents

ILLUSTRATORS 23

SEVENTIES

(70 TO 79 POINTS)

As a flower child, you can't help expressing yourself—whether through art, music, or close conversation. Being touchy-feely extends to your home, too: you love the indulgence of fur (just make it faux), a shaggy rug, or a super-loungy sofa.

Indeed, Tom Wolfe coined the term "the me decade" to describe the seventies, when folks were disillusioned with the Vietnam War, and turned their attention to themselves and their families. Nature-inspired neutrals mixed with bright Technicolor splashes as patterns became zanier than ever: you basically wanted to ogle everything in the room.

CHILL OUT, MAN

- Groovy wave or floral prints
- Earth tones with a dash of red, turquoise, or goldenrod
- L-shaped sectionals to create conversation pits
- Lots of texture: shag, faux fur, felt, macramé
- Teakwood
- Curvy chairs like the iconic Egg Chair
- Hanging plants and terrariums

BOHEMIAN
(80 TO 89 POINTS)

You leave no room for fuss or rules. Why? You're simply too busy layering your textiles and making sweet love to your Moroccan poufs. You consider yourself a creative type—an artist or writer (by profession or just in practice) and your look is usually flowy and easy, layered and casual, with global vibe.

Because Bohemians have a hard time curtailing their hobbies, multipurpose decor is a must. Want to meditate? Here's an oversized pillow. Taking a walk? Grab the sarong on the sofa. When guests pop by, floor pillows, ottomans, and occasional tables come to the rescue.

OFF THE BEATEN PATH

- Worn rugs and upholstery
- Intricate global patterns
- Handmade tribal accents
- Indoor hammocks
- Distressed furniture
- Hand-dyed linens and fabrics
- Strong, saturated colors on furniture and textiles
- Patterned dhurrie poufs
- Tropical indoor plants

MODERN GLAM (90 TO 99 POINTS)

Welcome to Hollywood. To you, all the world's a stage, and we are simply your audience (and hopefully your guests). If someone calls you a drama queen, you take it as a compliment because you are theatrical, glam, and larger than life—and so your home should be, too. You can't stay away from luxurious throws, bold colors, and ornate patterns, and if given the chance, you would cover your walls in a red lacquer that matches your lipstick. So what are you waiting for?

Modern Glam morphed from Hollywood Regency, which was born of 1930s movie sets that had to be loud enough to look luxurious in black and white. Thanks to the fabulous starlets who brought home the decorating inspiration, the trend spread quickly. Rich and luxe, overexaggerated, heavy, and saturated are key to this style. The focus is on feminine curves, metallics, luxe finishes, and generally just bling anywhere and everywhere.

LIFE IS A CABARET

- Lacquer walls
- Plenty of bling from chrome or brass
- Really big statement mirrors
- Luxe fabrics like satin, velvet, and fur
- Bright graphic wallpapers
- Asian details and motifs like chinoiserie and bamboo
- Chandeliers dripping with crystals and brass
- Velvet ornate furniture
- High-contrast color palette with lots of jewel-tone accents

TOTALLY EIGHTIES

(100 TO 109 POINTS)

You're all about having fun and dancing in the streets—you only live once, after all. You take risks and flock to eccentric shapes and crazy color combos—it wouldn't be unlike you to set a vintage beanbag chair under your Warhol print. As Andrew in *The Breakfast Club* reminds us, "We're all pretty bizarre. Some of us are just better at hiding it, that's all."

While eighties interior design is remembered for so many tacky details (an overkill of mauve and chintz), it also had some fun moments and art deco influences that can look youthful, vibrant, and a little out of control—in a good way.

JUST ANOTHER MANIC DECADE

- Neon lighting in any color
- Glass and brass dining tables or coffee tables
- Colorful pop art
- Mirrored furniture
- Geometric patterns with an art deco bent—a scallop or triangle
- Round-arm upholstered furniture
- Pastel colors—they are back, folks
- Luxe fabrics like patent leather and plush velvet

RUSTIC (110 TO 119 POINTS)

Life is simple, and you wouldn't want it any other way. For a natural homebody like you, nothing beats a long hike in the woods followed by a dinner at your reclaimed table with veggies plucked straight from the garden. Country style is set up to feel like a home away from home: always cozy, laid back, warm, lived in, and comfortable. Casual patterns like stripes, plaids, checks, and floral are all common in these spaces. It's like the house that Ryan Gosling's character built for Rachel McAdams's character in *The Notebook*: chock-full of romance.

RELAX, YOU'RE ON VACATION IN BIG SUR

- Furniture with an aged and beautiful patina
- Red- or blue-stripe pillows (especially ticking stripe)
- Cotton or linen slipcovers
- Sofas with deep seats and padded arms for afternoon naps
- Washed linens
- Wildflowers cut and arranged in an ironstone pitcher
- Cast-iron or copper accents
- Pretty, old hardbound books
- Rustic wood floors

TRADITIONAL

(120 TO 129 POINTS)

You're like the oldest sibling of all the personalities—dependable and an upholder of traditions. You often reminisce about the past—the way things used to look. The chaos of the modern world makes you crazy; instead you long for black-and-white movies, old hardbound books, rooms softly lit by candlelight.

A Traditional house is warm and inviting, with an air of sophistication. The set of *Downton Abbey* is a (very luxe) version of what this style used to be, but the house in *It's Complicated* is a modern interpretation called New Traditional.

AS IT ALWAYS WAS

- Persian rugs
- Wingback chairs
- Crystal chandeliers
- Antique tea sets
- Classic patterns like damask, chinoiserie, or matelassé
- Tufted headboards
- Gilded accents
- Alabaster lamps and marble busts
- Oil portraits or landscapes

STYLE WHEEL

Just like a color wheel, the style wheel below will help you choose looks that mingle well together, simply by finding a style's opposite. The wheel progresses clockwise, from the most scaled-back styles (Scandinavian and Minimalist) to the most ornate (Traditional). Remember those first two questions you answered at the beginning of the quiz? Those helped determine which side of the style wheel you sit on. Here's a tip: If your results fell in the mid- to high range of any style, you probably have a tendency toward its adjacent style, too.

Now that you know your design personality, find it on the wheel and check out its complement.

Because the two styles are so different, they'll look the best together. Take, for instance, Traditional. With its tufted-back chairs and ornate wallpapers, it might be tricky to combine with another very detailed style like Spanish or deco. Balance it with minimalist elements, like from Mid-Century Modern, which sits opposite to Traditional on the style wheel. Try a retro slim-lined sofa with some more traditional floral and fringe throw pillows. Grab a traditional Persian rug and add Danish modern armchairs—the combo is both unexpected and yet easy on the eye. As you get comfortable with these two styles, try adding another style until you find the right mix.

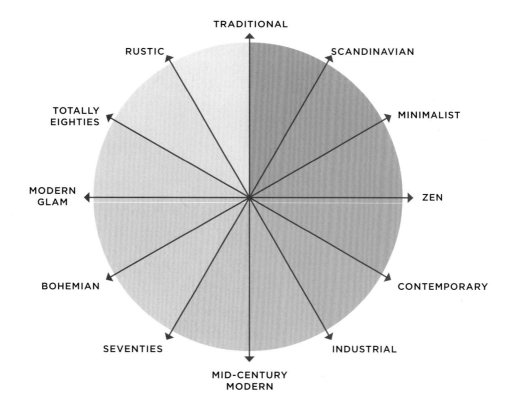

02

INSIDER
speak

STYLISTS ARE LIKE KARAOKE SINGERS—
THE LESS FORMAL TRAINING AND THE MORE
GUTS THEY HAVE, THE BETTER.

You know that eager chick who can sing Whitney Houston's "I Will Always Love You" perfectly? No one is interested in emotional vibrato at the karaoke bar on Taco Tuesdays. Just sing "Sweet Home Alabama" like it's your last night on Earth and bring us to our knees. Similarly, being great at styling doesn't require an expensive design degree, just a bit of practice and a dose of desire—or in my case, obsession and confidence. But while I don't believe creating a beautiful room entails following a dogmatic set of dos and don'ts, there is some lingo that's helpful to know when you're first getting started.

VIGNETTES

A VIGNETTE is a smallish arrangement of objects or furniture, usually including pieces that reflect the personality of the person who lives there. You'll hear this word over and over in this book and generally on the Internet.

On a magazine shoot, our goal as stylists is to show information about the design of the space but also tell a story about the people who live there. The photographer captures the room as a whole—in what we call a pulled-back shot or an "overall"—which is important, for sure. This kind of shot helps you understand the room layout, composition, and the overall color scheme, but you'll also want to get in there closer to know more about the person who lives there. So the photographer will always get tighter shots that show off the more intimate details and what makes this person unique. This is where a stylist starts obsessing—and we do obsess. We make the most of these moments, creating beautiful, self-contained stories to tell you, the reader, how interesting these people are. Vignettes are your secret sauce to a well-styled room.

VIGNETTES: YOUR SHOW-AND-TELL

When you invite people into your home, you want them to see who you are. Often, what tells them that isn't your couch; nay, it's your weird country milking chair that sits under a vintage portrait of a man who might be either happy or drunk. This particular vignette tells people more about you than many other pieces could. For instance, do you have a secret dream of being an Olympic cow milker? Or are you just simply inspired by strangely shaped chairs that reference another time?

You want your guests and friends to know about your interests. While you could blab on and on about yourself, you're better off letting your favorite objects and mementos tell those stories for you.

IT'S *SO YOU*

The biggest compliment guests can give you is to say that your home is *totally you*. You want them to see your personality as soon as they step through the door, but that's not going to happen *only* through big pieces of furniture. Your sofa may be tufted or velvet, but it won't tell the complete story about where you've traveled or what you're into specifically. On the other hand, a corner styled with a vintage guitar and a few framed rock records takes your story a bit further, helping you express your love of Led Zeppelin.

Creating self-contained worlds around themes or with a collection of littles you love will result in a beautiful, highly personalized room that guests will immediately pick up on.

style secret As you go through your things and decide what to play (or decorate) with, help yourself to a tip I got from my first stylist boss: "Pretty always goes with pretty." Generally if you love something and it's pretty, you can make it work with other favorite pieces (especially if it matches your color palette).

TIME TO OBSESS

Create one vignette, and I promise you'll find it a teensy bit addictive. You'll start obsessing over the details (in a good way), and you might even choose to refresh your vignettes rather than rearrange your space when you want an easy room update. When I get tired of the style in my bedroom, instead of redesigning it, I restyle it, then, boom! My room feels brand new, and I didn't move a piece of furniture.

HONE THE DETAILS

Once you lay down a few vignettes in a room, make sure they "speak" to each other and don't compete. Ask yourself three questions:

- Does one vignette look more heavily styled than the others?
- Do any vignettes lack color or details compared to the others?
- Are there any surfaces you haven't addressed, like a corner or a side table?

Start moving things from one vignette to another so that everything feels harmonious and the details are evenly "peppered" throughout the room. This does not mean you need to cram your room full of accessories—it just needs to be balanced.

When you think about creating multiple vignettes, you end up with a space that looks intentional, well-designed, and full of your personality because every area and surface—even the corners—is considered.

4 vignettes to drool over

To get you started, here are some of my favorite vignettes to style. Play around with these ideas, and substitute objects that you already have.

1 Warm and Cozy Reading Nook

A sleek recliner outfitted with a nicely folded wool blanket and a lumbar pillow, a side table for holding a glass and a book, and an oversized rolling lamp so you can get just the right light.

2 Go-for-the Gold Bar Cart

Plenty of pretty liquor bottles and sparkling water, a shaker filled with flowers, and decorative glasses that match the cart—use one of them to hold a few tools.

3 Sunny-Morning Sofa

Poppy colored pillows (skip the hand chopping!), a casually draped throw, an arc standing lamp, and a colorful side table holding a splayed-open magazine.

4 Keep-It-Rustic Coffee Table

A stack of simple art books topped with a modernist sculpture, a wooden tray that holds everything from coasters to remote controls, and a favorite photo under a magnifying glass.

CONTRAST

CONTRAST is the combination of opposite elements in a room, such as styles, shapes, colors, patterns, sizes, and textures.

The amount of contrast you have directly correlates with the amount of "energy" you have in the room. Simply put: A room with a lot of contrast will feel more energetic and busy, and a room with less contrast will feel more calm and quiet.

Get the contrast right and get ready for compliments like, "Oh my, isn't this room just so relaxing, I just want to curl up on that low-contrast chaise and have monochromatic dreams." Or the opposite: "OMG, hi!!! Your house is so fun, your face is so big, you have so many colors, I'm not going to sleep for days!" I find that most people fall somewhere in the middle—they want their rooms to feel interesting without looking insane and quiet and without boring them to tears.

You can create contrast in a room through six elements:

- Style
- Pattern
- Color
- Shape
- Size
- Texture

Choose the amount of contrast for your room based on your personality as well as on functionality.

HIGH CONTRAST

OPPOSITE When you want to take more style risks, think about doing so in your more "temporary" spaces. You're less likely to get sick of the design in these rooms:

- Powder rooms
- Guest rooms
- Kids' rooms
- Mudrooms
- Hallways
- Dining rooms
- Entryways

LOW CONTRAST

THIS PAGE Opt for a quiet, restful mood in rooms where you'll spend more time and want less visual noise:

- Your bedroom
- Potentially your living room, if you're the type of person who uses it as a refuge

ignore
your color
instincts

If you love color, *don't paint your walls*. It's counterintuitive, but here's why: if you have a tendency to buy lots of colorful accessories and you also have color on your walls, then your room *could* look like a crazy person lives there. With my color obsession, I know I have to stick with white walls, wood, and brass finishes, or it would just be too much color and pattern everywhere. By keeping the foundation of your room quiet, you give yourself permission to layer on the chaos, and the result is graphic, lively, and colorful without being too busy.

If you love muted tones, *use color in a bigger way*. Paint an accent wall or buy a large solid-colored rug. Remember that your instincts will be to shop for and to layer on objects and accessories in a "safe" color. A bright, happy hue like peacock blue or a slightly more saturated neutral heather gray will help you avoid a beige-on-beige-on-beige room. And I don't care how color shy you are—nobody wants to live in a beige room (except for really boring people, which I know you are not because you bought this book).

CONTRASTING STYLES

As you discovered in the last chapter, you're not just one style and your room shouldn't be either. Keep in mind that opposites attract: Styles that are the most different actually look best together, and mixing any of them with streamlined or modern furniture usually keeps them looking fresh. For instance, if you only mix Moroccan with Spanish—two very ornate styles known for their inlaid, carved furnishings and lots of detailed tile work—the styles look *too* similar, and you'll end up with a room with a lot of competing pieces, where nothing catches your eye and the style looks too Old World. I love to mix one style that is more decorative and ornate with a cleaner and more minimalist style, like Mid-Century Modern. If you have a lot of South American fabrics, then think about combining them with a simple French grain sack stripe, instead of an ornate damask; with a little less going on in one, the details of the other sing.

Mix as many different styles as you want, just limit the amount of color you bring in. Seven wildly different styles can work in a room with a very firm palette. But multiple styles in twenty-five different colors? That's been done and is called "schizophrenic non-chic." It's not trending and it's not coming back in.

style secret Quickly switching up your room's contrast is more difficult with an insanely patterned wallpaper or hot pink sofa. So keep those larger, more permanent surfaces quiet and bring in contrast through fun accessories and smaller decor.

CONTRASTING TEXTURES

So you want your room to feel lived in, collected, and storied, but you also want it to be very calming? Every room should have contrasting textures. If all of your furniture were upholstered in the same fabric, it would be like wearing a denim jacket and a chambray shirt with jeans—no offense, Canadians. It's just too much and your eye wants some relief. So when you're choosing materials like velvet for your sofa, spring for linen or leather on the side chairs. Mix up the fabrics for your throw pillows (wool, velvet, silk, cable knit, or metallic).

With lots of different textures, keep your color palette limited to a few different colors. If you have eight colors in a room and you layer in too many bulky textures, then the room can start looking a little heavy.

TONAL OR TONE-ON-TONE

TONE-ON-TONE involves styling different tones of the same color together.

Tone-on-tone is the Coco Chanel of room styles. Classic, quiet, iconic. And like Coco's advice about pulling an outfit together—"Before you leave the house, look in the mirror and take one thing off"—so too with a tonal room. This less-is-more look works best in the bedroom. If you are going for a tonal look, follow these three simple tips:

- Don't go OCD and pick only tones on the same paint swatch. You can push the color palette until you find your eye jumping to a color in the room (believe me, it'll stand out like a sore thumb).
- Include a wide spectrum of some darker tones and some lighter tones.
- Don't forget texture: mix in plenty of shapes and different fabrics to keep it interesting.

COLOR PALETTE

A **COLOR PALETTE** is a selection of colors for a designed room.

The color palette is one of the most essential elements in your room, and while you know what the term means, I know that when it comes down to identifying colors you're going to live with for a very long time, you've probably gotten stuck once or twice. Follow these five steps for the best color palette ever:

1 **Find the color you love putting on your body the most.** The biggest hint about the main color you should decorate with is hanging in your closet. The hue that keeps popping up most often is the one you probably feel most confident around. Use it as the jumping-off color for the rest of the palette. That is not to say that if electric blue is in fashion this year, you need to paint your walls that color; it just means to take a cue from what you love to wear. If you're drawn to a lot of blues, think about incorporating that color into the space. If you find yourself never wearing purple, then maybe it's not for you—in your fashion or in your home.

2 **Add a highlight and a lowlight.** Ever had your hair highlighted before? You'll notice how the lighter and darker shades work together to create depth. Highlights are brighter and a little bolder and add punch; lowlights are more pulled back and subtle and help ground everything. Add variance to that one big color you chose and bring in one lighter, brighter hue and one subtle, softer hue that complement your main color. If your main color is French blue, then maybe your highlight is teal and your lowlight is heather gray. If your main color is pink, then your highlight could be a brighter fuchsia and your lowlight champagne.

3 **Don't stop at just three colors.** A room with a small color palette may be easy to understand, but it can look like an uptight person lives there.

4 **Mix in warm tones and cool tones.** Every room has to have a mix. Include both warm tones (reds, oranges, yellows, browns, and beiges) and cool tones (blues, greens, grays, whites) to create balance in the room. Surprise yourself by springing for colors you aren't typically drawn to. And remember that materials like wood, gold, and silver count, too (wood and gold equal brown, silver equals gray).

5 **Choose one fun accent color.** Add a color that you can take out or change whenever you want. It should sit far away from your main color on the color wheel (like a very happy yellow to a masculine navy) and can be very bold. Think: hot pink, flashy coral, or bright kelly green. Just like that chunky necklace that you are obsessed with for one season and can't look at the next, keep your accent color flexible and replaceable. In other words, don't paint your beautiful hardwood flooring in the Pantone color of the year.

DESIGN MYTH

Think a small room looks bigger with dark paint? Nope. It doesn't mean that it won't look good, but dark paint will just make it seem small. This is a proven fact; ask every woman in America. Everything looks smaller in black—even our rooms.

LAYERING

LAYERING involves placing items in front of or behind others to create a collected look. It can apply to vignettes or whole rooms.

When a stylist arranges the furniture, accessories, and textiles in a way that creates depth and texture, the result is a layered room that looks like it's been lived in and loved for years—even if it's just a staged set. You see items in the foreground and background, up high and down low. Every space feels appropriately filled out—even if it's minimalist. But you don't look at it and think, *I'm suffocating, I can't find one pocket of air to breathe from.* Nay.

One of the keys to layering is knowing when things are too perfectly placed; it'll feel like a robot designed your room. So give yourself permission to let loose a little.

By working things on different planes, you'll create the illusion that history is in play, as if your stuff has been collected over time. You'll also fool anyone into thinking you're a natural—as if you just threw everything together already knowing how great it would look (even if you rearranged it ten times, or forty).

style secret If you're a minimalist, leaving all surfaces in your house unadorned is not an option if you want it to feel like a home, but keeping them tightly decorated is. It's all about adding larger-scale accessories in the foreground, background, and on surfaces. Instead of a gallery wall, think one big piece of art. Instead of a collection of miniature gold shoes (what?), think about getting a huge, simple gilded vessel.

my rule of 3s

The rule of threes is no secret—it works for writing, photography, and design, and it's a great trick for layering vignettes. Presenting information in threes makes a grouping more memorable, but you have to include variety. Trying to look at three similarly sized objects at once is too chaotic—they compete with each other. (It would be like looking at a parade of floats that are all similar in size, style, and color—after a bit you are super bored, of course, but more important, you feel like you're going insane because of the repetition.) Your eye wants a bit of variety in order to decipher what's really happening. So I've come up with a super-easy, you-can't-lose rule. For every surface (be it a mantel, console, coffee table, or dresser), add these three things:

• Something vertical
• Something horizontal
• Something sculptural to tie the two together

For a mantel vignette, you might choose a vertical piece of art and a horizontal stack of books. Then you'll want something that connects those two to soften the jump your eye makes from a vertical to a horizontal plane. So always include a bridge, an object that has more organic, sculptural lines. A vase of soft peonies might be all you need.

Instead of placing three objects next to each other with the same amount of space in between them—which will looked too propped, like a store display—arrange one in front of another to create depth and then move the third one off to the side, giving the trio a bit of room to breathe.

BALANCE

BALANCE is visual equality of objects and furniture in a room.

Balance is key to creating a room that's calming and not visually chaotic, but don't get bogged down by this term. Your eye tells you when things are right. What you really want is for things to look balanced even if they aren't physically the same.

If you place a large floor lamp on one side of the sofa, then you need something on the other side so the sofa doesn't look like it will tip over. But don't go out and buy another lamp. Mix it up: Try a small standing vase with flowers on a side table with a larger piece of art hung behind it. The vertical line of the vase and the art will balance the scale of the lamp. Again, you're striving for *visual* balance, so don't assume that each piece needs to have exactly the same weight.

SCALE

SCALE is the proportion between your furnishings as well as how they fit in with the rest of your room.

Here's a simple guide: If you have a big house, buy big furniture; if you have a medium house, buy medium-scale furniture, and if you have a small house, buy smaller-scale furniture. It's really that simple. If your sofa is huge, don't buy a tiny side table for it; buy a large-scale side table.

How do you know if everything is the same scale, especially when you're out shopping? Keep in mind these tips:

1 Your coffee table should be at least two-thirds the size of your sofa. If your sofa is at least seven feet long, your coffee table should be around four to five feet. Love that pouf trend? Use one as an accent table or in a corner, or two as your coffee table.

2 The height of your furniture should be similar. As a general rule the arms of your side chairs should be a similar height to your sofa arms. Your side table should also be a similar height so you're not reaching over the side of your sofa too far to set down your drink.

3 If you have a big room, then buy a big rug. Going too small is one of the biggest mistakes I often see, and it can really ruin a room. If you have a large living room, then you'll need at least an eight by ten if not a nine by twelve. I know that five by eight sounds big online, but once it's in your space it will look teeny tiny.

4 If you have a small room, go for smaller furnishings. Otherwise, the room will feel cramped and lose most of its function. Settees and accent chairs are easy to rearrange, so you can get more uses out of the room than you would with one massive piece. If you want a sectional, choose one with slim lines that doesn't add to the square footage.

FOCAL POINT

A **FOCAL POINT** is the area of the room where your eye first lands when you enter.

Walk into a well-styled room and you'll find yourself immediately attracted to one area: the focal point. Styling your focal point gets you the most bang for your buck, as it's the first impression guests will have of your room. Can't figure out your room's focal point? Hint: It's normally something obvious, like some architecture in the room—a fireplace or a set of huge, beautiful windows. Otherwise, it's the most dominant wall—probably the one you face when you walk in. Bingo. That's where you should hang that upholstered headboard or oversize mirror.

Keep in mind that your focal points don't need to be wild statements. While they are important and give you a style foundation, I'm not suggesting you go build an altar in the middle of your living room. You're just trying to draw the eye and give it an entry point to discovering the rest of the room.

MOOD

MOOD is the atmosphere or feeling of a room.

The first question I always ask my clients is, how do you want your space to *feel*? They get to choose three words. When you walk into the room, what feeling do you want to wash over you? Happy, giddy, amused? Blissful, cheerful, refreshed? In the beginning of your process, finding three words to give voice to your room's atmosphere is more important than deciding what it should look like. They provide the framework for all of your shopping, organizing, and styling decisions. And when you're trying to choose between two sofas, that little voice will tell you to go with the comfy one because that's your goal. My three words are "happy, airy, and exciting." I constantly have to remind myself of that when picking out pieces, and it seriously works.

Next, think about spaces you've been to that fit your vision. If one of your descriptors is "flirty" and your former best friend in NYC has a really glamorous space, think about the highlights. Is it her diamond tiara collection? Her metallic leather headboard? Her velvet chaise longue? Then you can replicate her secrets (reflective surfaces, luxe textiles, high-end-looking furniture) in your own house.

03

in ten easy steps

NOW THAT YOU KNOW YOUR SIGNATURE STYLE
AND SOME KEY INDUSTRY TERMS, HERE'S A QUICK
RUN-THROUGH OF HOW TO STYLE YOUR ROOM.

This chapter is brief, because let's be honest—the best way to style a room is by stealing ideas from photos and re-creating them in your own home, which is what the next section is all about. But there are important steps to follow to get your room ready for its close-up.

STEP 1: Keep It or Chuck It

Time to play my favorite game: keep it or chuck it. You learned what really jibes with your style, so now you can comb through your home and decide what doesn't belong and what absolutely has to stay. Maybe you're a minimalist and your home is already edited to its bare essentials and you're ready for Step 2. Or maybe you have hoarder potential and need to focus hard on this step before moving forward.

Take the temperature of your nostalgia about each piece: if you were to lose X, Y, or Z, would you miss it after a week? Or would you melt into a puddle and bawl at its loss? With most things, the decision is not that black or white, but for five seconds pretend it is and notice what reaction you have. You might be surprised.

If you're ready to go whole hog and completely redo your room, try keeping enough travel mementos and beloved items so that your room won't feel like you decorated it in ten minutes. As we've agreed, you want to create a sense of history in your space, like you've been collecting and adding to it for years (and with some styles, even generations). Aim to keep a few large and medium pieces along with some small accessories to pepper your personality around the room. Most of all, clear off all cluttered shelves and other surfaces so that you can start with a clean slate and create cute little vignettes.

editing tip When I move I assess everything in these three categories: beautiful, functional, or sentimental. Everything should be at least one of these things, and if you live in a smaller space, then it should be at least two of these things.

STEP 2: Make a Mood Board

Collecting your inspiration can help you style your room in a cohesive way. But the hard part is always translating the beautiful photos and swatches to a room that already exists. Here are my easy tips:

- Clip with abandon—don't edit yourself just yet. Pin paint chips, magazine tear sheets, and fabric swatches on poster board or add it all to Pinterest. Name your board something like "What I like a little, love a lot, and want to put in my mouth because I'm so obsessed with it."
- Now balance your clippings. Are things looking too feminine or too random—maybe not even you? Rearrange, edit, add, and re-pin at will.
- Revisit the style wheel to add photos that reflect your complementary style. Then consider if the photos reflect the function of the space: For a more energetic room, bring in lots of color contrast (think black and silver or navy and white) and tons of colorful accessories. For a low-key look, add more texture and tones.
- Edit your pins to be more realistic in terms of your budget and your time. Save some pins for a rainy day.
- Take photos of your mood boards with your phone or transfer your swatches into a small notebook so that when you shop you can be sure that colors and materials match.

color tip **When I'm looking for a good paint color, sometimes I'll just Google it. A search for "ice blue paint color" will turn up dozens of suggestions from decorating magazines and websites.**

STEP 3: Set the Stage(s)

Step back to focus at once on all of your furniture and on textiles like rugs, pillows, and curtains. Is everything in tune with your style, or do you need to switch out a few pieces? A few style tweaks might make all the difference. For instance, in your living room you might:

• Consider whether a new coat of paint could do wonders (I promise, it will!).

• Check that your furniture is arranged for the best possible "flow." Make sure that your sofa and accent chairs are conducive to conversation.

• Change your curtains for a new style or just take them down if you have a great view.

• Get a new (or vintage) rug. Because they take up so much visual space, you'll gain instant style.

- Add personality with a small accent chair upholstered in a fabric you love.
- Switch out your shabby throw and pillows for fresh styles. You'll be surprised at the difference it makes.

Once you're happy with the foundations of your room, find a few inspiring surfaces to style. These will be the stages for your styled vignettes; depending on how big your room is, you may want one in each corner so you can balance your styling throughout the room.

Clean off these surfaces, polish the heck out of them, or give them a quick refinish. Your bookshelves should be stripped bare at this time so you can consider what should really go on them (instead of what has incidentally collected over the years).

Divide the accessories you cleared off your shelves into two piles: one for Step 4 (to be future styling props) and one for Step 1 (to be chucked).

Here are a few of my favorite tips for bringing out the best in an oldie but goodie:

- To avoid (or just delay) having to reupholster a sofa that needs it, wrap a brightly colored quilt or luxe blanket around the seat for some color or texture.
- Update a traditional lamp by putting a new drum shade on it. It's insane how much this simple thing can modernize an antique.
- Give a vintage rug or an old, beautiful quilt a second life by hanging it on the wall (or headboard).
- Repurpose an antique dresser as a console or media storage for your living room or entryway.

STEP 4: Work with What You've Got

Don't go shopping just yet. You might already have everything you need to style a cute little vignette—if you look in the right place. Take the time now to pull together all your pretty, interesting things. Maybe set them on the floor or the coffee table so you can see them all together. Without actually styling anything just yet, group together similar "props" (in style or color) that you might want to display as a collection. If you live in a one-bedroom or studio, don't worry about keeping kitchen things in the kitchen or the artwork in the living room. Let a beautiful piece of serveware such as a cake stand become the stage for a side table vignette. Here are a few of my favorite everyday props for styling that you might overlook:

- **Stash boxes.** These are both good fillers and good at being filled with things you want to hide.
- **Sculptural objects.** Don't overthink this. Every surface is dying for a pretty sculptural object to help it.
- **A tray.** Trust me, every room needs a tray to hold a bunch of little things together.

organizing
(or starting)
your collection

Are you a natural collector but feel no one actually notices your collections? Maybe it's just a matter of organizing them so they make sense to the eye. For small items that won't stand up on their own, consider framing them, either together in one large frame or separately, to hang them as a gallery wall. For a large collection of items, come up with a catalog system so that you can keep the best on display and store the others away. Then when you get bored, you can easily switch them out for a brand-new look.

Don't have a collection yet? Here are some tips for getting started without getting overwhelmed:

- Think about what you might want to collect before you even start shopping.
- Let one thing that speaks to you at a flea market inspire a whole collection.
- Remember that you don't have to be obsessed with something to collect it—you just need an appreciation of its shape or story.
- A collection can be as ordinary as they come; the simplest and cheapest items look the best when displayed en masse. Even spoons can look beautiful when displayed together.
- Identify what you're really into and then research items that might represent it. If you love Julia Child, you might collect vintage French salt cellars.
- The more specific the item is, the more interesting, though if you go too esoteric, you risk not being able to grow your collection without spending a lot of money and time.
- Don't collect every single teacup you find—make sure there is something unique and special about each item in your collection so it adds to the whole and doesn't just take up space.

STEP 5: Now Work in the Weird

Every room needs something random to pique interest, give people pause, and keep the room from looking too perfect. You probably already have those things. Look around. What's the first thing people comment on when they walk in? Is it the large drawing of a blimp that you got from the flea market? Or is it the wire sculpture face of a woman that is both engaging and terrifying? What interest or obsession sets you apart?

Figure out that quirk and embrace it. It's what will keep your home from looking like it was plucked straight from a catalog. And it's what will keep the room interesting *to you*. If your room bores you, then it will totally bore everyone else. Collect these things and add them to your pile of styling props.

STEP 6: Go Shopping

By now you should know what's missing from the stuff you already own. It's those pretty details like flowers and an objet d'art that you sprinkle in with the rest of your collections to make your home really come alive. For magazine shoots we stylists always bring in *a ton* of books, plants, art, lighting, vessels, objects, pillows, throws, frames, and yes, even food. The number of pretty glass (and often French) water bottles that I've purchased is uncountable. And lemons—but not just any lemons. Lemons with leaves on them so that I can style those leaves to ever so naturally fall over the lip of the beautifully hand-thrown bowl. Learn this, future stylists: Everything looks better in a more natural state—chunky rustic loaves of bread, wooden crates, or even some books with their jackets removed to show their pretty linen surface.

STEP 7: Start Playing

Now is the time to style your first vignette. Turn on some music to get your creative juices flowing, and start by tackling just one corner or surface. Give it your full attention before you move on to the next one. While this is the fun part, it might take you longer than you think to get it right. Reference the lessons you learned in Chapter 2 to create your first vignette with contrast, using my rule of threes. Once you finish one vignette, move on to the next, keeping in mind how it might relate to the first one (remember, you're striving for balance throughout the whole room).

While it's easy to obsess over details in this stage, try to keep things from looking too perfect. Don't hand-chop every pillow or fold your throw too nicely. Let it all hang a little loose and casual so it looks like you actually live there (and so guests don't feel too uptight). Stylists even want the water carafe or jug of juice to be either one-third full or two-thirds full, but *not* half full (ha!) and certainly not all the way full. That's not "natural" or "real life." Two-thirds is my personal favorite, and yes, I'll pour out that extra one-third to get it. It's a bit OCD, but worth the effort.

STEP 8: Capture It on Camera

Once you finish styling your room, you can take a step back and look at your work, but the only way you're really going to focus on what could use tweaking is by capturing it on camera; this is one of the most objective ways of seeing your space. You don't even need a fancy Canon to do it, either. Use your smartphone (then if you love the photo, you can easily share it on Instagram).

Once you have your shots, load them onto a computer if you can—it helps to see the details enlarged. Take notes on what you see—does one corner look too cluttered or minimal compared to the others? Would one vignette be better on a different surface? Should the flowers come to the center of the room? Keep a running list of what you want to change. After each shot, I ask myself, *If you, Emily Henderson, saw this in a magazine would you stop and think it's a beautiful room? And if not, why?* Then I fix it.

nice shot

I turned to my amazing interiors photographer David Tsay for his dos and don'ts on how to snap interiors with a smartphone. Here's what he said:

- Do take photos of the room at different angles: whole-room shots while standing in the entrance, straight-on shots of a piece of furniture, and close-up shots of your vignette at a three-fourths angle as if you're peering right into the collection.

- Do turn off all the lights. Different lightbulbs give off different colors and intensity, so it's best to shoot in natural daylight.

- Don't use your flash. Instead, invest in an inexpensive and lightweight tripod that fits your phone. Most of the time, your exposure will be slow without a flash, so this will help keep the image from blurring.

- Do plug in your earbuds if you have an iPhone. You can use them as a camera shutter so you don't shake the phone while snapping away.

- Don't fall back on ready-made filters, which can get boring because everybody uses the same ones.

- Do play with the photo settings. Instagram and other photo apps let you easily tackle enhancements that will bring more life to your shot.

- Don't keep them to yourself. Tag your photos with #styledthebook so we can see the results!

STEP 9: Edit, Edit, Edit

Now it's time to take off your stylist cap and put on your art director cap. A stylist never nails it on the first try, as she always has an art director breathing down her neck, changing his mind or coming up with a new idea. Now it's up to you to decide what needs editing, improving, and scaling back. Take a few things out of your vignettes, then snap another photo, and compare the two. Which is better? Rework your styling, being as judicious as possible.

STEP 10: Refresh Your Space

There. You did it. And you'll love it for maybe . . . a week. Maybe longer. But there is a chance you might get sick of looking at that needlepoint pillow of the Space Needle or vintage animal mask collection every time you walk into your living room. Lucky for you, styled vignettes are not permanent fixtures like your sofa or coffee table might be. You can—and you should—switch up the details whenever you want.

Refreshing the styling of your home is the quickest way to redecorate and make your space feel new again. The best part? You don't have to buy a thing if you don't want to. It's all about rearranging, editing, and curating your look for the way you want to live. Now it's time to have fun with some decorating porn. Keep flipping for the world's biggest collection* of my styling ideas, tips, and tricks I've learned over the years.

*This hasn't actually been verified. I called Guinness and they are still getting back to me.

STYLE SECRETS FOR
EVERY ROOM

living rooms

THIS SPACE IS LIKE YOUR HOME'S BUSINESS CARD, SO MAKE IT MEMORABLE.

As the main spot where your guests will spend time when they come over, your living room is what they're most likely to remember after they leave. Also, as one of the biggest rooms in your home, it has lots of planes for styling; and this chapter covers them all, with tips for the coffee table, the bookshelves, the side table, the sofa, and even your television (yes, that's right. Sick of looking at your TV? Turn to page 150). Go all out and give your living room lots of love so that the impression it makes is a lasting one.

KEEP IT CALM

If you think neutral means boring, you haven't met this living room. This neutral color palette becomes more interesting with the layers and layers of texture and contrast. Notice there are no huge splashes of color—nothing really jumps out at you—yet you are totally drawn in. Every room needs a combo of both round and square shapes for variety: Here a round pouf, round side tables, and the organic shape of the coffee table relax the square shapes of the club chairs, rugs, and the sofa.

A. Matching side tables create a uniform stage for different lamps.

B. The larger lamp is farthest from the entrance so it doesn't block the view.

C. Different pillows and throws help the matching chairs feel collected.

D. A leather pouf punctuates this large space and throws off some of the formality.

E. The black in the palette is muted by soft fabrics, light neutrals, and slate gray.

F. A tucked-in striped throw brings tailored preppiness to an ordinary sofa.

OPPOSITE While this tablescape looks collected and effortless, there is a color palette working hard here: blues, greens, and taupes evenly peppered in the books and vessels speak to each other, pop against the dark background, and make the randomness feel cohesive.

‹ why this works

A side table is one styling opportunity you don't want to miss—but overdo it and your guest will have a hard time finding a place for her drink. Here's what the designer did to create just enough interest:

• She brought in a pretty box to separate the black lamp from the black table.

• To keep the vignette coherent, she styled a black object on the black table and a white object on the light wood box.

• The finishing touch is a coaster that has major style and looks great even when the glass is whisked away.

restoration home   mark & sally bailey

DARRYL CARTER | THE NEW TRADITIONAL

STEVEN GAMBREL

DOMESTIC ART   ASSOULINE

CABRIOLETS   JEAN-PAUL THÉVENET
PETER VANN

Oddball sculptures like a pair of fists, a goat, and black-and-white cubes all of a sudden look sophisticated in neutral colors, while a trailing plant helps connect the two shelves.

1 sofa 4 ways

Your sofa might be the most stressed-about purchase in your home—besides your dining table and bed. If you're in the market for a sofa and don't know what style is best, you can be sure that going for something gray, comfortable, and clean-lined will be the best decision you can make. Its surrounding details can be tweaked slightly for a refresh or completely overhauled for a brand-new room. Check it out:

1 Candy-Colored and Pop Contemporary

This ordinary sofa takes on femme charm under a bright, oversized painting. In fact, all of the pink in the color palette tricks your eye into thinking the sofa is more lavender than gray. A few luxuries, like Mongolian fur, Lucite tables, and fashion books, make the sofa a sweet spot to chat with the gals.

2 Black, White, and Warmed Up with Wood

A two-toned color palette and a few natural masculine materials (tusks, wood, and leather) turn this living room into a grown-up bachelor pad. A gray velvet sofa softens harsh black and white colors, while a big use of graphic patterns keeps it modern.

3 Romantic Boho with a Touch of Traditional

Surrounded by a tonal color palette, a gray sofa looks perfectly at home in the country. Quiet, simple details thrive—a white ruffled pillow, a tasseled throw, clothbound books—and you instantly feel like you've left the city to start your vacation.

4 Cool Coastal Mixed with Classic Americana

All of a sudden this sofa looks young and Portland-cool. Faking out a little vintage allure with a new sofa is easy to do when it's raised on slim wood legs—one of the features of mid-century furniture. Surround the piece with flea market finds, such as a stack of old suitcases, and a collection of found sea paintings, and you've just made yourself look interesting.

BRILLIANT IN BLUE

A deep saturated turquoise wall (in high-gloss paint, no less) instantly makes this mix-and-match living room feel slightly dressed up and traditional. To help emphasize a more buttoned-up look, designer Taylor Jacobson introduced symmetry through matching lamps, side tables, and chairs. But special touches keep it relaxed and welcoming: worn leather, a simply shaped sofa, a driftwood coffee table, and a Souk shag rug. To avoid an overly eclectic effect in this minimalist space, every color accent connects to something else: the wood tones in the coffee table, frames, and shades; the red on the sofa and chair; the brown in the rug and the leather chairs.

A. A gallery wall is hung to look like one big piece of art.

B. The center point of the collection is at eye level.

C. The art starts ten inches above the sofa so that heads won't hit any of the pieces.

D. The height of the side tables is perfect for reaching for your drink.

E. Lamps are at a convenient height for reading (about sixty inches from the floor).

F. The red flowers, blanket, and accent chair perfectly complement the turquoise wall.

OPPOSITE Every shelf on this side table is styled differently, but they share the same color palette. To vary the look, the designer styled two stacks on the bottom shelf, one stack in the middle, and a collection of littles on top.

photo tips **(THIS PAGE)** When photographing a large single piece, it's important to pay attention to what's going on around it, too. Here's how we approached this chair photo:

- Be mindful of objects in the background competing with each other; this lamp doesn't visually touch the piece of art.
- We included the basket on the side so your eye wouldn't abruptly fall off the right side of the chair.
- A blanket on the arm of the chair breaks up the dark leather and brings the color of the wall forward in the frame.
- A feminine color palette of turquoise and red is balanced with masculine neutrals, such as beige and wood and leather finishes.

Sometimes a bookshelf really is just for books. I like to line up all the spines of the books evenly about an inch or two deep into the shelf. The result appears more organized, especially when you are dealing with so many different sizes and colors of books.

bookshelf basics: 4 fun vignettes

The number of blog posts and videos I've done on bookshelf styling is uncountable. It's perceived as hard, and I get it. Your bookshelf is probably the most difficult piece in your living room to organize and arrange because of its many surfaces. For the majority of folks, it can be a bit of a dumping ground for books, DVDs, or random treasures brought back from vacation that you can't think of anywhere else to display. Time to pony up and style these intimidating suckers. These four vignettes show that styling your shelves doesn't always have to go "by the book."

1 Have Some Control

While your initial reaction might be to add books and other platforms to help ground a shelf collection, another (almost opposite) approach is arranging small art objects in a flat grid. It's an easy way for your eye to read each piece. It works just as well, but is best on a lower shelf where it can get full exposure.

2 Hang in There

Try hanging artwork between shelving to add dimension and break up the monotony of stacks of books. Be sure to call the artwork out; a wooden chain draped over the frame and a clip lamp both work hard to highlight the piece.

3 Use Your Words

Cool typography prints with witty sayings, quotes, or mantras will pique a guest's interest in your bookshelf, maybe more than a particular book might. You can go classic like, "Keep Calm and Carry On," or you can go for something new, informal, and modest (so you won't get tired of it quickly).

4 Keep It Tight

Remember: a bunch of little things will look more organized if they are in a small color palette. Use each shelf to feature books and accessories in one or two colors. This classic Scandinavian collection looks neat and collected in white and wood.

MORE IS MORE

This living room is meant to comfort the maximalists out there and prove that it is possible to live well with more. While this room has so much going on, every detail has been thoughtfully placed, from the throw to the artwork to the globe collection on the shelves.

A. A large sisal rug grounds the conversation area.

B. A small, colorful kilim rug was layered on to add color and personality.

C. Two portraits that feel balanced because of their similar colors and size flank the shelving.

D. A grand bookshelf helps fill the high ceiling and serves as a focal point behind the sofa.

THIS PAGE This statement horse lamp flanked by two colonial rattan chairs suggests a conversation area next to a window. To keep things traditional, match both your chairs and throw pillows. But too much symmetry is boring—so make sure these pillows have great personality.

photo tip **(OPPOSITE)**
Shooting an open window always makes a room (and a shot) more inviting. It breaks up the lines of the window frame, lets in more light, and makes the room feel happier. Be careful of too much backlight, however; you still want to see the details inside.

When you have a large collection, like these globes, it's always nice to showcase them together, but add other objects and books to keep the vignette fresh. Paintings hang between large shelves to fill empty space, while vintage objects like wrestling helmets and bowling pins also act as sculptures.

gallery wall 101

A quick Google or Pinterest search will give you dozens of ways to hang a gallery wall, including the complicated process (which I've even blogged about before) of planning your gallery wall on the floor by tracing your frames on paper before hanging it all up. Well, here's an even easier way to get that added-to-over-time look:

- **Collect all of your art.** You don't have to arrange it in a certain order, just take stock of what you want to hang.
- **Find a place that will hold all of your art.** A collection of art looks best if it fills the entire wall, so find the right balance between your space and your art collection (and maybe pick up a few more frames for your latest travel photos).
- **Make sure you have many different sizes of art to work with.** From the super-large abstract canvas to four-by-six-inch (and even smaller!) frames, variety helps.
- **Collect art of different orientations.** You want and need vertical, horizontal, square, and even round to create the most dynamic gallery wall.
- **Find your anchor piece.** Decide which piece is the one you want your eye to jump to as soon as you walk in the room. Hint: It's probably one of your larger pieces.
- **Hang your anchor piece off center.** This important trick keeps the anchor from overwhelming the rest of the gallery wall so all of the pieces work together as if they were one.
- **Start hanging the rest.** Based on the position of your anchor, begin hanging other pieces by alternating between large and small so every size is evenly spread around.
- **Watch your color balance.** Make sure you're not hanging all of your black-and-white art on one side and color on the other. Sprinkle the color equally throughout the grid to keep your eye moving around.
- **Don't limit your art.** Allow it to spread along the entire wall—from sofa to ceiling and corner to corner. Don't be afraid to hang high or really low.

Collecting art is like watching TV midseason: When it's good, you can't get enough of it, so fan that addiction hard and marathon without shame. But when it's bad, you should try to pare back a bit and focus on other things until that stellar fall season lineup is back.

STRENGTH IN NUMBERS

This is the blockbuster of grid art walls: full of drama and romance, like men with long hair wielding swords while privately acting vulnerable. It's epic and wonderful. Vintage botanicals, all framed exactly the same way and hung in a floor-to-ceiling and wall-to-wall grid, create incredible drama and impact. We should all try this look. The stripe pattern on the daybed mattress has just the right small scale to contrast with the large botanical grid, which, in a way, acts as an oversized pattern. Every detail in the room is there to emphasize the botanical motif.

A. Oversized green pillows anchor the daybed.

B. A collection of small pillows avoids an overly symmetrical arrangement.

C. Matching lamps with square bases and shades echo the rectangles on the gallery wall. The symmetry is striking.

D. Two occasional tables are paired together to make one coffee table.

E. Flowers and a dramatic fur blanket give presence to the sofa so the paintings don't overwhelm it.

This vignette is kinda magic. Velvet pillows, a fur throw, and wooden sofa details echo the soft, organic motif of the botanicals.

HI, HANDSOME

OPPOSITE The grand curves of a Chesterfield sofa and modern floral pillows soften a moody space that calls for sipping Scotch in a crystal lowball glass while watching PBS. Masculine touches are styled throughout, including a grid of framed daguerreotypes and a cowhide sofa pillow. Two antique columns become pedestal perches for collectibles (of masculine busts to match the theme, obviously), which are set off by glass domes that catch your eye right off the bat.

A. Next to a sofa styled to the max, a warm throw sits on the ottoman at the ready for colder nights.

B. Though a contrasting pattern, floral print pillows still harmonize with the rug because of their similar colors. Sometimes the harsher the contrast, the better.

C. A plant is that sculptural piece needed to bridge the sofa and the columns and soften the entire room.

THIS PAGE The designer curated a few curiosities on these pedestals and gave them a gallery look by adding glass domes. Bell jars instantly elevate everyday objects into artwork and create small worlds for your guests to explore. In Beyoncé's words, if you like it, then you shoulda put a dome on it.

portraits: face to face with my favorite art

Hand-painted original portraits are a traditional style of wall art, one that dates back centuries, but they don't have to feel ancient in a modern home. In fact, I find that they add plenty of personality to a wall (literally), if only because faces instantly draw a reaction out of you. Bring home a portrait or two with these tips:

- Do find cheap paintings in the junk pile at flea markets. Give the frames new life with paint.
- Don't go commission a family portrait, necessarily—unfamiliar faces bring new energy to your room.
- Do go for a quirky over a precious style—something that makes you wonder what the subject is thinking or that makes you smile.
- Do judge a painting based on its color palette; find one that comes close to the scheme of your room.

- Don't spend money on a frame if the canvas is wrapped—the undone look is totally downtown atelier.
- Do hang multiple portraits in the same room so they mix and mingle (but don't talk out loud to them).

FRESH PREP

This room makes me want to join a country club. This serious tufted leather sofa takes on English country ease with two unexpected black-and-white plaid accent chairs. Just because you have a long sofa doesn't mean you need to fill it completely. Sometimes a sofa doesn't "want" a lot of pillows. In this case, the designer used only two pillows on one side and a throw on the other. The two pillows are fairly light in visual weight and the blanket is heavier, so the result feels balanced.

A. A sleek, simple coffee table quickly shifts a classic sofa toward modern.

B. A plaid throw and patterned pillow mimic the accent chairs, helping the sofa relate.

C. The entire collection of furniture fits on one rug. Success.

D. The round tray contrasts with the large square coffee table.

E. This neutral rug still has a lot of texture and color variation.

F. Blue lamp shades are loud enough to call your eye to the side of the room.

One of my favorite color palettes is blue and gold, which perfectly complement each other, as they sit far apart on the color wheel. One is super masculine and dark while the other is feminine and glitzy—it's as if George Clooney and Cate Blanchett got together. Look how awesome those lamps look in that combo. Black side chairs keep your eye on the lamp shades. While black and dark woods are not usually partners, black books on the credenza make the chairs seem more intentional.

OPPOSITE Here's a dramatic corner vignette with a single piece of awesome. The 1960s leather Plycraft lounge chair and ottoman engage the whole corner—it doesn't need much else (except me in it, pretending it's mine).

THIS PAGE If a piece of art isn't very wide, place it off center so it doesn't look dwarfed on your console. Speakers can be a dude's best friend but a stylist's eyesore; a planter in a similar color softens the effect.

MODERN MARRAKESH

Welcome to Relax Town. Population "dunno, don't care, I just want to be there." When you start with a Scandinavian base of white and cream with lightweight furnishings, the opportunities for a nuanced style become endless and therefore exciting. Here, the layers speak to a global influence with the camel sculpture, pouf, and woven baskets. Everywhere you turn, comfy touches abound, from the wild fur draped over a chair to the navy cotton velvet upholstery to the sprawling low-pile rug. Best of all, *nothing* distracts from a gorgeous view of the Silver Lake hills—no TV, no drapes, not even too much art. You know when you've got something good—no sense in taking away from it.

A. In a warm-weathered room, a fur is that fun detail you wouldn't expect.

B. Skip the TV above the mantel, and use a unique conversation piece as the focal point.

C. A long table calls for multiple but simple vignettes to fill it out.

With a long coffee table come plenty of opportunities to show off your personality. Go beyond the basic books and flowers and bring in oddities that only you know you like. A tic-tac-toe game is at the ready for the kids to pick up and play with, while a Popsicle-stick basket shows off a skill learned at summer camp. A memento from the nearby beach, a piece of driftwood, sits proudly on top of two art books.

NOTHING
BETWEEN
US

ONLY SKY
ABOVE
US

OPPOSITE If you're a minimalist with collector tendencies (or have a partner who is, bless his heart), try keeping all of your pretties in one contained space. A built-in bookshelf is just the space for letting yourself go—but make sure you keep some kind of method to the madness. Here, books are ordered by color with some shelves reserved only for objects. Remember, keep it in the same color palette and you are one huge step closer to style success.

THIS PAGE The area just outside the living room serves as another space for hanging out. An all-weather rug, a water carafe, some easy-to-care-for plants, and a cozy throw are all you need to connect your outdoors to your indoors.

the fireplace mantel: before and after

Ready for some styling sleight of hand? You might not notice the subtle changes we made to this mantel at first, but the styling is significant enough to make a difference. Here's what we did:

- We brought the speaker and vintage records to the left side of the frame to balance the fireplace wood and tools.
- We spread out the collection of candlesticks just a bit.
- We draped some ivy over the mantel to fill the fireplace's negative space.

- We changed out the small bird figurine with a low horizontal basket—the bird felt bitsy on the long mantel.
- Don't worry, we kept the bird and moved it atop a collection of books that we beefed up to balance the right side of the mantel.

Voilà! Styling magic.

THIS PAGE His and her styles can live together, as shown by this pretty white piano juxtaposed with animal hides. If your taste leans more feminine, make sure to tone it down with a few masculine details.

BOHO NATURALIST

OPPOSITE Some people like a lot of stuff and some people just don't. If you're not one to be light on stuff, you might as well embrace all of your "crazy," your wonderful things, and your eccentricities. I sure have. Here's a great example of how this bohemian did it right. A hammock even takes the place of a side chair—talk about makeshift seating! In this maxed-out space, warm colors layer on top of cool colors and Southwest patterns on the sofa mingle with a Moroccan dhurrie.

A. When your style is as wild as this and if privacy is not your concern, skip the curtains so the focus stays on everything else.

B. A trio of triangle art and tall lamps and plants draws your gaze up to the extra-high ceiling.

C. A favorite blanket covers the sofa for a super-casual vibe and fun pattern.

D. The crowning achievement isn't a chandelier but a large branch studded with bulbs, a fitting choice for this room. This house is in Oregon, after all.

RETRO RANCH

Combined with large-scale antique cowhides, a mid-century monotone room feels perfectly relaxed in this ranch-style home. When you love wood grain as much as this homeowner does, use it as a main color in your palette and pepper it with warm accents, like ruby and cream.

A. A runner in the same pattern as the main rug connects the walk-through space to the living room.

B. A double-shelf table gives you double the surfaces to display your things.

C. Two identical lamps hold together a display of different vessels on a long console and add symmetry to this eclectic assortment of wonderfulness.

THIS PAGE A low lounger and a storage credenza are a perfect pair on an unused wall for an extra reading spot or just a place to contemplate the honest truth about L.A.'s obsession with juicing. Oversized artwork, coffee table books, and an indoor garden are an easy invitation to hang out. You can also store your latest romance novel, a throw, an extra pillow, or any other extras behind the credenza's doors to prolong your stay.

OPPOSITE To freshen up a mid-century aesthetic, an arc lamp and worn textiles soften all the geometrical shapes—the coffee table, the art frames, the stacked side tables, and sofa arms.

A round coffee table fits perfectly
in the space in front of this rounded
sectional. Styled with oversized plants
and art books, it becomes visually big
enough to match the scale of the sofa.
That's what styling does—it changes
your perception of things by changing
the context.

photo tip Bags and shoes aren't
just for entryways—sometimes they are
just the thing to signal a cozy spot to
hang, as if you just couldn't wait at the
door to sink into that grand sofa.

how to hide that tv

Everyone has them. We all watch them. But why let that huge black rectangle suck up all of the decorating energy in your room? Make the most of your media with these tips that help take the focus off the TV and maximize your styling space:

- **Include it in your gallery wall.** Hang art in a similar color palette all along the wall that holds your TV (see page 120 for tips on hanging a gallery wall). It's even better if you have black frames, which will help the TV blend in. Before parties, upload a pretty landscape photo that looks like part of the collection.
- **Surround it with shelves.** Mount your TV on the wall or set it on a credenza, then bring in shelves on either side to create a focal wall (Ikea's Billy bookshelf system has plenty of wide and skinny options for fitting shelves perfectly to your space). Style those shelves with objects and art, and that TV will have a hard time hogging the spotlight.
- **Paint or wallpaper the wall.** A dark color will camouflage the television so well that you'll have to turn it on to find it. Make sure that any furniture on that wall is white and bright so that you have some contrast in the space (you don't want the wall to look like a black hole).

- **Hide it behind artwork.** This involves some installation, but if you do it right, you can easily lift the framed piece off the TV whenever Netflix comes a-calling. Make sure your art frame is deep enough to cover the entire TV (I suggest about five inches deep). I've built frames like this out of furring strips (find them at Home Depot), then I attached a French cleat system to the frame and the wall. As it is a bit of work, this is for the hard-core DIY people who really hate their TV.
- **Prop a pretty screen in front of it.** If your TV is hanging on the wall and you have the floor space, spread out a folding screen to block it from view. Then when friends come over for movie night, voilà! The screen comes up and a TV appears.
- **Cover it with a beautiful textile.** Go for something vintage and handmade, like a beautiful quilt or an antique tapestry. Attach rings to the piece so you can slide it aside to watch TV.

05

ENTRYWAYS, CORNERS, AND
creative spaces

**BRING THE FUN BACK TO FUNCTIONAL IN
THESE HARDWORKING SPACES.**

The entryway, mudroom, and home office take a big beating—
they're where we drop our stuff but are often the last picked
for the team in the game of decorating. How sad. Why not
take some risks and make these spaces useful, energetic,
and stylish? Show your friends that you have major design
aptitude by giving those smaller spaces the attention they
deserve. Here are solutions for prettying-up a hallway credenza, organizing your entryway, and staying inspired at your
desk, so you can finally tell your boss you're working from
home (on a Monday that just happens to be the first snow day
of the year, no less!).

CREATIVE CATCHALL

You're most likely to drop the most important things at your entry, so why not stay organized with a console that has storage inside and a surface on top? A table lamp is best for welcoming you home late at night (it's so much nicer than keeping on an overhead light). Rather than a last-look mirror, I love how this homeowner hung a large piece of art—inspiration as soon as he walks in the door.

A. A pretty trash bin serves as a stealthy way to stash junk mail.

B. Leaning a piece of art in front of a larger piece of art feels casual.

C. The branch helps bridge the tall lamp and clipboard to the horizontal artwork.

This entryway tray holds a collection of well-appointed boxes and smaller trays that keep keys, coins, mail, and wallet looking pretty and organized. A decoupage cup holds glasses to grab on the way out.

< **why this works**

This little architectural niche includes a few functional and pretty details to welcome home the resident. Here's the thought process:

- A small tray holds a leather pouch, keys, and a vase with something pretty.
- A blanket breaks up the length of the bench and creates a soft spot to sit while taking off shoes.
- See how the leather—on all three bags and the shoes—warms up the space.
- That artwork—it's just plain rad and makes guests smile as they leave.

THIS PAGE Create an unexpected mini-gallery in your hallway with artwork hung from floor to ceiling. A soft tonal rug keeps the space feeling big but still textured.

the credenza: styling from start to finish

Whether in a hallway, living room, or dining room, a credenza can help keep your stuff orderly, while also presenting a huge opportunity to show off your styling smarts. We played with a few props on this credenza before settling on a storied, layered look. Here's what we did:

1 We cleaned everything off to start with a blank slate.

2 The pieces of art were the most important, so they went on first, with the piece on the right hanging out by itself.

3 We added contrast to the credenza with a contemporary lamp and styled more details, including a wood bowl, books, and a vase. We swapped the portrait for a frame in a contrasting size.

4 In the end, we arranged all the elements closer to achieve a mountain-range effect. The finishing touch: a few feathery flowers to connect the artwork to the objects.

PRETTY USEFUL

OPPOSITE The mudroom on the left is not spare by any means, but there is a place for everything: shoes, bags, scarves . . . it's even ready for the weekend with blankets and a basketball for the park.

A. A built-in bench is a gracious way to ask guests to take off their shoes.

B. A mix of pillows anchors the corner of the bench.

C. Install two levels of wall hooks all the way across the space so guests have plenty of space to hang their stuff.

D. Folded blankets hide their edges to keep things neat.

E. A tray that corrals wallets and keys is a must, even with no console.

F. Clear empty bottles fill the last cube without adding clutter.

THIS PAGE Sometimes you just have to take it off as soon as you walk in the door—in that case, hooks always help. I love how this bag invokes everything we look forward to at the end of a long week. And even a necklace draped over the doorknob speaks volumes about how this person decorates: Nothing is so precious that it needs to wait for a formal arrangement. Get that cool piece on display ASAP, before you pass out from chic exhaustion.

PREPPED + READY

A classic little nook is outfitted with items that anyone would love to grab on the way to the beach or a Saturday in Malibu. If you don't have a proper entryway, you can still designate a quiet corner to hold all of your essentials as soon as you walk in the door. Just grab a pouf or a stool and a floating shelf, then make it yours.

photo tip Bags, shoes, and sweaters give photos a sense of your personal style, while also showing the function of furniture.

KIDS WELCOME

An entryway that leads right into a kitchen nook stays organized and out of the way with a bench and a basket to contain clutter and give support. The chalkboard is just for fun. No reminders or fancy chalk art here—only kids' sketches, games, and autographs welcome.

A. A basket that holds magazines and junk mail gets triple points for looking rustic and handmade. Nice job, basket.

B. A bench pillow goes a long way in coaxing guests to take off their shoes.

C. No ordinary kicks here—these shoes show off the homeowners' fun, casual style.

D. The chalkboard ledge acts as a shelf for the art and photo strip.

E. A tall branch from the backyard looks like an oversized floral arrangement.

6 goodies to welcome you home

Coming back from a stressful day is hard enough with traffic or a long commute, so treat yourself to these creature comforts as soon as you walk in the door:

1 **Cheap and cheerful blooms**
This is a given—it's something we all know will make us perk up, but a luxury we tend to pass over.

2 **A plush rug**
Give your rug the touch test before you bring it home. The one for your entryway should feel lavish—almost like a welcome-home hug for your toes.

3 **A console**
Go for storage or just surface, but either way, this piece will serve as your own personal butler (and keep you organized on the way out).

4 **A bench or two side chairs**
Taking your shoes off at the door will help make that fresh mopping last a little longer. But guests might overlook your cue if not for a comfy seat near a tidy pile of shoes.

5 **Artwork**
Express yourself and create a big first impression. Go for the quick win: something bright and happy. Your mother will be impressed.

6 **A chandelier**
A chic chandelier is an investment you'll be happy you sprung for. While the installer's at it, have him add a dimmer switch so you can create just the right energy for your mood.

LASTING IMPRESSIONS

OPPOSITE This entryway makes me want to get to the flea market early in the hopes of catching finds like these. A vintage post office box used as a console holds a collection of objects and who-knows-what tucked away in dozens of drawers. The styled surface is a study in artful arranging—perhaps not so functional for an entryway, but memorable nonetheless. Besides, why lay out the mail when you have your pick of storage?

This carved stone antique lamp takes on a much more modern tone with the square drum shade. Pairing it with the Fornasetti piece might seem risky, but we loved the whimsical repetition of faces on the table—almost like two guests at a party, mingling, flirting, and finally exchanging numbers.

A. A leather dog leash adds to the ruggedness of the drawers.

B. The umbrella on the right creates symmetry with the leash.

C. "See no evil, hear no evil, speak no evil" figurines create drama with their repetition.

D. The seventy-plus drawers don't look so busy because they disappear into the wall.

MODERN LIBRARY

OPPOSITE This homeowner installed shelving to transform a corner into a mid-century-style library. The shelf was designed to look built-in, with a finish that replicates the wooden walls, but brass vertical braces give it some glam and contrast. Books alternate between horizontal and vertical—some are even leaning so it feels more effortless and thrown together. The finishing touch, a stylish seat, is at the ready for any eager readers. Just read something cool, won't you?

A. Vintage speakers are balanced evenly (but not too evenly) around the shelf.

B. A mix of books and objects helps the library feel less serious.

C. True to mid-century style, a few plants bring a little of the outdoors inside.

D. Books sit up, lean on their side, and lie flat to make the library look like it gets used.

THIS PAGE A soft, trailing plant helps offset the squared-off masculine shelves.

THIS PAGE Nobody puts baby in a corner. With curves that look lush in black leather, this modern chair takes the wing style to a whole new level. Set beside a telephone desk with an arc lamp, it becomes an ideal spot for devouring a pile of art books and magazines.

ALL CURVES

OPPOSITE In case you're wondering about the best place to set up an office, it's right below an open window—one this high gives enough light to keep you energized, with any distracting happenings just out of sight. This desk totally found its BFF with this chair— they both feature curves up top with angular legs below. A few sculptural office accessories that match the polish of the chair and the tight color palette help reinforce the glam. All that's needed is an awesome job to match this cool space.

A. The curlicue arms perfectly contrast with the desk's arrow-straight lines.

B. This dark ink blue matches the color of the molding.

C. This gold lamp is angled directly at the gold chair, tying the scene together.

D. A Japanese maple branch lightens all the heavy woods and fills the corner.

E. The orchid's pink, a warm highlight, holds the color palette together.

desk details:
how to stay organized and inspired at home

Working from home doesn't have to feel so lonely—it's all in your approach. Whether you use the space for catching up after hours or receiving and winning over clients, treat yourself to nice details and a little inspiration, and I'm sure you'll find your productivity soars. Here are a few ideas:

1 Think outside the box with organization essentials that come in the form of a beautiful hand-carved wood bowl for business cards or an old leather dice cup for holding pens. Never underestimate the power of a small tray on the desktop; it will make your surface look collected and classy. Finally, a luxe tape dispenser might seem superfluous in the store, but just watch the look on your clients' faces when they get insight into how much style you have.

2 Do *not* forget the family when setting your office hours. Not only will photos of them relax and rejuvenate you as those hours grow long, but they'll also show clients that you have a human side (and prove to your fam who really comes first). Skip the frames on a small desk and spring for anything that clips or props up the photos—in this case, a few fun wooden clothespins.

3 If your workspace has a lot of stuff, keep it tucked away so you know exactly where to look. In this case, vintage file boxes and lock cases are flea finds with plenty of function (even better if you have the option to keep the drawers labeled). Extra supplies (notebooks, Wite-Out, and pens) are stacked neatly and at the ready. A little just-for-fun motivation comes in the form of a small "Go!" print.

4 With a beautiful bowl full of cherries, some peonies, and a few acrylic paintings, how is any work getting done here? You'd be surprised! Don't stop at the smart stuff when organizing your desk; bring in a little inspiration and personal expression to let your mind wander in order to solve those tough creative problems. Experiment with things you love and see how they transform your work ethic.

THIS PAGE Rethink the window: Rather than covering it with curtains, go bare but lean a few pieces of artwork on the ledge to enhance your view. As for the desk, any large table will do the job; dress it up with footed bowls for a feminine touch.

photo tip When shooting a horizontal photograph, try styling similar colors along the "horizon" of the shot to create a landscape effect. Here the blue bowl, paintings, and flowers keep your eye moving across the shot.

FANTASY FREELANCING

OPPOSITE Swinging is not for everyone, but this writer wanted a whimsical space that would inspire her imagination, so she installed a swing for much-needed thinking breaks. Who would ever turn down an afternoon of brainstorming while in midair? Naturally, the swing adds whimsy to this grown-up space and sets the tone for this homeowner's creative career. The pouf is basically an adult-appropriate bean bag that contributes more comfort and playfulness to the space.

A. Tall branches make a natural statement without overpowering the space.

B. The chair is turned toward the door to make guests feel welcome.

C. A large painting in quiet neutral colors engages the whole wall without cluttering the room.

CORPORATE COOL

OPPOSITE Why wait for that promotion? Create your own corner office in an unused nook with a huge piece of wood and sturdy braces. In this case, filing cabinets act as the desk legs and in black, they disappear. Place a worn vintage rug down for integrity and pattern—and a little comfort to remind you that you're still at home.

A. Black and white make a very smart palette for a home office.

B. We used a vintage birdcage ladder to fill this vertical space and add whimsy.

C. Gold accessories say art deco when juxtaposed with a classic palette.

D. This plant helps balance the lamp on the right.

THIS PAGE Hang a flag in the window for an architectural shape that also shades you from the sun.

READING RAINBOW

People love to organize their book collection by color, and here's an example of that done right: that is, on an expansive set of shelves with every color represented. The icing on the cake is the lime-green chair and yellow-green flowers that pick up on the colors from the middle of the bottom shelf.

A. The white desk accessories echo the bottom shelf of white books, helping to visually balance the darker books up top.

B. A super-chunky desk lamp matches the novelty of the color coordination.

C. A ceramic balloon dog is not a typical styling prop, but one that lets you know this homeowner has fun.

D. Two shorter shelves give extra surface without being in the way of work.

THIS PAGE Bud vases look best when clustered and elevated with small books of a similar scale. Just a few simple stems are all the vases need.

WORK OF ART

OPPOSITE When considering where to carve out a home office, remember that you don't need too much square footage. This tiny workspace in a living room was created out of a built-in with a larger shelf installed as the desk. Lots of art helps the office sit well in this room, but a coat of paint on the back wall makes it feel like a separate space from the rest of the room.

A. This chair is an accent in the living room that doubles as the desk chair.

B. This task lamp is visually big enough to balance the painting on the left.

C. Black boxes "zigzag" down the shelves and visually relate to the task lamp.

D. Centering this peculiar eye sculpture in the middle of the vignette gives a bull's-eye effect so you know what to look at first.

E. Light wood shelves make the space feel larger (darker shelves would have stopped your eye from traveling upward).

F. A fern plant reaches to the ceiling, which draws your eye up.

MIX PLEASURE AND BUSINESS

OPPOSITE Dark rustic wood paneling sections off this home office, which is cleverly surrounded by built-in cabinets. Sconces are a smart option in the office, as they free up space on your desk while bathing it in light.

A. You don't have to hardwire sconces. These plug-in ones work just as well, plus their braided cords look chic hanging down.

B. This grid of art is uneven and interesting, but aligning the bottoms of a few pieces keeps it orderly. Centered between the sconces, the collection visually creates a square.

C. Playful figurines such as horses suggest preppy equestrian style.

D. The lavish touch of a marble top makes this office nook feel permanent.

photo tip **(THIS PAGE)**
An overhead desk shot is a really fun styling opportunity to show off just how organized you are to your social media followers. A few of your personal items like sunglasses and a photo strip prove that you don't take things too seriously, while a to-do list gives your fans insight into your daily routine.

SMART SYMMETRY

The interior designer who lives here knows how to create balance without boring us. The desks, chairs, and stools perfectly mirror each other, but the background is a wildly decorated landscape of art and inspiration. A swing hanging in the foreground is another creative detail in this awesome atelier.

A. Use a picture frame to contain your inspirational photos and clippings.

B. A vintage hexagon-shaped light helps center this area.

C. A plant hanging from the shelf feels bohemian and casual.

D. This large collection of vases creates depth by bringing your eye to the edge of the room.

E. The subjects in the paintings are facing the same way, weaving order through a busy scene.

F. A simple clip light from the hardware store is elevated by the chic collection.

The surface of a long, low shelf is just the right space to showcase a large collection of objects, like these vases. An inspiration board is where you want to organize all of your creative clutter, and a heavy frame helps keep all of it collected—visually and practically.

photo tip Make a collection more dynamic by displaying the taller objects in the back and shorter in the front. Then style together shapes that complement each other: On the left are hourglass-shaped vases and on the right are ones with wider necks.

06

KITCHENS AND
dining
rooms

THE ART OF HAVING PEOPLE OVER IS
ABOUT *THEM* HAVING IT ALL.

What better way to entertain than pulling together a cheese plate arranged on a rustic cutting board, some wineglasses that looked plucked from Italy, and a few French linen napkins? But styling the kitchen and dining room is more than just decorating—it's also about creating a sense of abundance. It doesn't matter how beautiful your space is; if your dinner party guests aren't comfortably seated with their glasses full and food within reach, you can be sure they'll start thinking about an exit plan. As you start planning these spaces, keep your most uptight guests in mind and you can be sure your place will be the most popular on the block.

KITCHEN'S OPEN

If you want to get your kitchen countertop in tip-top shape for guests (or a photo shoot), a few easy tweaks will elevate it in a way that is still helpful to your everyday needs. In this vignette, different cutting boards layered in front of each other warm up a stark kitchen. The mixture of wood, marble, glass, and pottery adds secret texture and depth to this vignette—you don't notice at first, but if all of the materials were the same, the countertop would look flat and boring.

A. A water tray anticipates guests' needs so they don't have to rummage through cabinets.

B. A cutting board relaxes the vignette while adding a little height.

C. This stool invites your guest to sit while you fix her snack.

D. Plates and bowls in neutral colors keep glass cabinets looking tidy.

Two layers of glass help enhance the sense of space: In these cabinets, art is placed behind clear glassware, which draws the eye to the back of the shelves. Art in cabinets is also an unexpected conversation piece that doesn't take up valuable counter space.

photo tip Opening cabinets for a shot is an old stylist secret. It lets the viewer easily see what's inside without any reflection.

IMPROVING
YOUR VIEW

A windowsill might be an obvious place for a plant collection, but a vignette like this will look as though it's been growing for years if you approach the space like a theater set rather than a police lineup. To keep the eye moving, pots sit on wood blocks—the varied depths of the vessels create different "scenes" in the display.

A. A plant gets the VIP treatment with a glass dome.

B. Warm up a black-and-white palette with natural fibers and wood, which help soften any masculine space.

C. No green thumb? Start with succulents—they need light but are hard to kill.

D. A Turkish hammam towel adds a central pop of color, pulling your eye into the vignette.

E. A plate elevates and contains the dish soap and lotion.

(C)

(E)

∧ **why this works**

You're probably more used to seeing countertop vignettes in still-life paintings than on Instagram, but they are so easy to put together . . . why let the masters have all the fun? Here's a little insight into our styling for this shot:

• We repurposed simple pieces of pottery such as saltcellars and spoon holders to keep the space organized, beautiful, and very functional.

• Instead of styling everything on a few flat plates, we included three different heights of platters and pedestals.

• Placing pieces in front of each other creates depth and invites your eye to explore the vignette.

OPPOSITE This amazing industrial store bin is now repurposed as a bookshelf, which creates a graphic and smart storage piece. These color-coded books look neat yet exciting, while anything else in there could have seemed messy. We added huge branches to the island to help separate the kitchen from the living room.

THIS PAGE If you have pretty dishware that you don't use every day, displaying it is better than keeping it hidden away. This perfectly spaced collection of Fornasetti plates looks like one large piece of art. A vintage water dispenser picks up on the shine in all of the plates.

photo tip We added flowers and plants to bring in some color, variety, and life here—otherwise the collection could feel like a store display of dishes. Keep an eye on your kitchen vignettes for this very reason.

BRIGHT, WHITE, AND WARM

Because we tend to have so many
memories tied up in the idea of a
kitchen—simmering stews, delicious
brunches, and holiday fêtes—you
want the kitchen to look inviting.
But white minimalist countertops on
white floors against white tile can
easily look flat, stark, and severe.
Enter you, the stylist. A few colorful
pots and vegetables put that
personal stamp on the space and
help liven things up.

A. If you don't use your kitchen that
much, arrange cookbooks and art on
overhead shelves.

B. A bright red Dutch oven and a Turkish
rug will make any visitor want to jump
right in and help out the cook.

C. Casually leaving out beets and
radishes from the market in a fresh
display gives guests a taste of what's
to come.

D. These Scandinavian-style stools are
minimalist enough to fit the space's
style with some wood tones to warm
up the room (white stools would have
disappeared).

E. Get creative in the kitchen: stemmed
artichokes make an appropriate
culinary "flower" arrangement that's a
delicious treat for later—plus they last
a long time.

start-to-finish styling: the kitchen island

If you're lucky enough to have a built-in island or the space to bring one in, make sure to give it the style treatment it deserves. Don't just stop at the basic decorative details like a bowl of fruit. Bring in accents that give other folks insight into your idea of a quiet afternoon in the kitchen. Here's what we did to get this kitchen island magazine-shoot ready:

- In order to emphasize the red and blue details in the kitchen, we set out red ovenware and crisp bread in neat packaging.
- A cute red purse seemed perfect for the nearby blue chair—it looks ready to be whisked away but in the meantime adds an extra dash of red.
- We brought in another rug for balance and extra comfort.
- Adorable polka dot mugs, a gold teapot, and a pulled-out stool are the final details that make you want to sit down and relax.

OPPOSITE With all of the horizontal lines in the paneling and dark window molding (although who would complain about that?), the branches were needed to soften the area. A cutting board provides a platform for propped bottles and glassware, and a casually laid-down tea towel connects the board to the counter.

THIS PAGE Here's an example of great styling for everyday use. A tray holds pretty fruit left out to ripen. Flowers are the eye-catcher that makes you smile every time you enter the kitchen. But don't stop at flowers—add a few plants: Terrariums are easy to care for and will last longer than a bouquet of blooms.

photo tip While white space isn't a bad thing, make sure your shot is perfectly balanced so that no holes distract your eye. With a diagonal line of objects in the foreground, we added a flower arrangement to fill the corner so that the cabinets in the back recede.

If only my meals were this dramatic. When cooking and eating happen in the same big space, don't feel like you have to keep it all white and lose the excitement of a moody dining room. On the contrary, this homeowner goes full-on fabulous with black cabinets and large swaths of magenta. The black pottery—a mix of high-end antiques and new big-box pieces—creates a dynamic collection that has plenty of impact and is more affordable than you'd think.

THIS PAGE Silver, gold, and copper accents elevate a simple white kitchen. The wood chairs and blinds act as warm, organic neutrals that pull the three metallics together. The black legs of the stools work perfectly with the black in the pendants, bringing a bit of industrial masculinity to this kitchen.

photo tip Copper is a perfect neutral for photos. These copper pots don't normally live on the shelves and countertop, but we wanted something that was soft, reflective, and not too busy to sit in the shot.

OPPOSITE Don't pigeonhole your art to the living room or hallway. Smaller pieces of art can live anywhere, and guests will be much more patient while you're cooking if they have an interesting view to keep them busy.

ORGANIC EATERY

Sometimes more is more even in kitchens. This artsy couple collects beautiful handmade everything—from pottery to macramé to canned goods. This one-of-a-kind look can travel from country to city—it's all in your attitude. In a Brooklyn town house, its calming mood would be the envy of every neighbor.

A. Keeping the Mason jars together offers an impressive landscape effect.

B. Trailing ivy is loose enough to match this laid-back style.

C. This hand-knotted macramé is eye-catching and large enough to equal the busy shelving on the right.

D. Arranging similar items together keeps the room from looking insane.

E. Curtains aren't necessary in a kitchen with a beautiful view.

THIS PAGE This simply styled table gets a boost thanks to a nearby banquette that offers extra seating and also serves as a storage buffet for napkins, extra dishes, and serveware. The pillows and artwork speak to the colors in the rug.

OPPOSITE This dining room is just so exciting. A few disparate styles come together in a similar color palette: A cozy seventies-style rug, mid-century chairs, and a traditional, ornate chandelier all share brown tones. Tall, sculptural plants help connect the dots of the styles and move your eye around the room.

TURN INSIDE OUT

If you are lucky enough to have an outdoor dining space, I command that you style it, love it, appreciate it, and *use it*. This space looks plucked straight from a European countryside, so we brought in amenities to suit. Artisanal cutting boards, a tray of craft beer, and a plate of delicious-looking pretzels are fun delectables for a fall gathering. An "all you can eat" sign in the corner is a tongue-in-cheek way to make guests feel welcome year round. Sit down and enjoy the brews, because Octoberfest isn't just for Germans (or just for October).

A. Extra logs near the woodstove stir thoughts of an outdoor fire and instantly make the space feel cozy.

B. Skip the flowers for an outdoor centerpiece—branches from the backyard are easy, cheap, and beautiful.

C. Wooden cutting boards and pizza paddles are natural outdoor accents (and make you look like a confident cook).

D. Lean art in an outdoor space so you can bring it inside in bad weather.

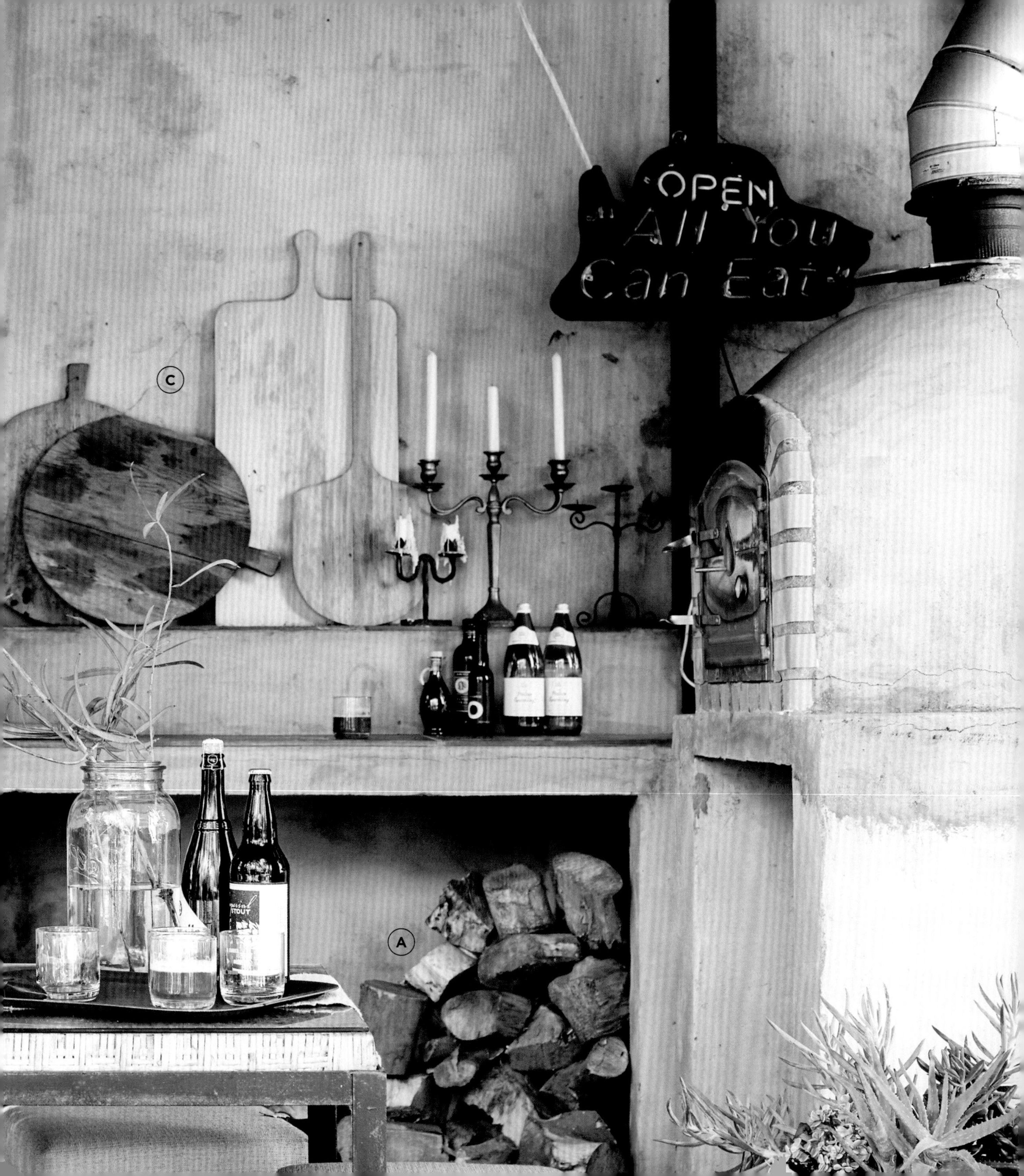
OPEN
"All You
Can Eat"
C
STOUT
A

WOOD WORKS WONDERS

So many people think that mixing wood tones is a design faux pas, but sometimes it's difficult to avoid with furniture you've collected and fallen for over the years. We don't live in matchy land, so don't be afraid to mix them up. When you start with white cabinets, lots of light, and not a lot of stuff, a mix of wood tones looks modern and fresh. Avoid any finishes that are too shiny or look fake or generic (like an "espresso" finish). From the chair legs to the table to the floors and every wooden accessory in between, this space makes room for all of it. Skip the rug in the dining room to let the floors shine.

A. Oval tables help the flow in "pass-through" rooms.

B. A glass chandelier is quiet but reflects plenty of light.

C. Nesting bowls arranged into a landscape form the centerpiece.

D. The black is the "color pop" here, bouncing your eye around the room from the wine bottles to the black bowls to the black on the stove.

THIS PAGE Nothing adds a twist to a vignette like a miniature object. Here a mid-century chair mimics the theme of the room. Check out dollhouse sites for versions of your favorite furniture, then style them on coffee tables, countertops, or even in terrariums. I even like to find the perfect miniature and place it under a dome on my bookshelves.

OPPOSITE With so much white space between the counter and the ceiling, just a few branches are a natural fit, plus the stems add another wood tone to the mix. Don't be afraid of stems— sometimes they can look messy but a few select branches will look simple.

photo tip   Huge branches offer insane splash for not much dough. They're so cheap (even free if you have a backyard), they last a long time, and they have a huge impact in a room. Go for the branches that are more sculptural instead of straight up and down pieces. The more organic and natural the shape, the better.

photo tip   A bike brings personality to what is otherwise a serious architecture shot and gives insight into how these folks live with their fabulous indoor-outdoor home. It says, "Hey guys, we just happen to have incredible taste in architecture and we are athletic and stylish in a really casual way."

how to add depth to your room

Creating depth is all about keeping your eye moving around the room so it doesn't get bored. This white kitchen was begging for some added dimension so the space would feel full (without looking overwhelming) and layered (like this person has lived here for years). It doesn't take much, but a few connected details will bounce your eye all over the room:

- For your biggest color, go with what's in the foundation of your room and then fill it out with similar-colored accessories. Notice here how the same tones—from the pendants and cutting boards to the floors—create a quiet base that still pulls your eye around the room.

- Add two or three unexpected doses of bright color to keep things exciting. Here, a bowl of lemons and a yellow pot as well as a blue vase act as highlights that your eye stops to glance at.

- Add some drama in the back corner. Styling a vignette in the corner has the same effect as the hot guy standing all by himself at the party. Folks just can't help glancing his way in case they can catch his eye. Farthest from the room's entry, the corner vignette in this photo makes you look all the way to the back of the room to check it out. He's available, ladies.

- Add some details near the ceiling to make you look up. This room has just enough space above the fridge to bring in a hand-carved wooden bowl. Serveware is best for these tight spaces—such pieces are nice enough to display and can be kept in a place you won't need to access every day.

- Pull out a chair. If all of the chairs are pushed in and out of the way, they could look too uniform and not very noticeable. But if you pull one out ever so slightly, it can make you glance at the interruption in repetition.

TRADITION WITH A TWIST

At first this gorgeous dining room takes on a very classic feel with a blue-and-white palette, an ornate wallpaper design, and antique chairs; but just look up and that uber-modern chandelier will suggest that you are in for quite possibly the best dinner party conversation you've ever had. Layering modern art details on a traditional canvas is a bold move, but when it's done in the same color palette it's absolutely adventuresome.

A. The ornate wallpaper works because the crisp white doors and windows keep it from becoming too overwhelming.

B. This chandelier pulls in all the colors of the room—blue, gold, white. I've never seen a chandelier that changes a room so much.

C. These see-through chairs are solid but not visually heavy.

D. A lofty plant in a gold pot is an impressive centerpiece for when guests arrive (and easy to remove when you're ready to eat).

E. White dinnerware keeps the table from looking too busy.

A dining room console doesn't take up as much space as a buffet and holds a few extras for the table: wine, candles, and a centerpiece.

OPPOSITE Just outside the dining room is a perfectly ordered bar with mixers, oranges, a cocktail tool set, and plenty of liquor to let guests know that their wish is the bartender's command.

THIS PAGE Glasses with different decals help guests keep track of which drink is theirs. Also, never underestimate what functional tools can do for the look of your bar—gold finishes match this pretty space and make these homeowners look like the craft cocktail bartenders they are.

set the bar: beyond the basics

A bar that's styled and ready to go as soon as guests arrive allows you to finish up any dinner details while they help themselves to drinks. First, make sure you have plenty of liquor options for all kinds of drinkers: Vodka, gin, and whiskey are the minimum requirements. Tequila, brandy, Scotch, and more will get you bonus points. Don't forget the fruit, soda, tools, and all of the appropriate glasses so they can shake and stir to their heart's content. Here are more ideas:

1 Trays help separate tools, liquor, and fruit so guests can find exactly what they need and corral all the tools. A cocktail book gives them courage to try that new artisanal manhattan all the kids are raving about.

2 Transferring your spirits into glass decanters makes them feel special, but be sure each one is labeled so you know what's what.

3 No area of your home is too precious to set up a bar. Here, a few coupes and liquor bottles sit on a cabinet shelf with lots of high-end art.

4 Don't try to cram it all on the cart. With no space to stash bottles, the ingenious homeowner installed a vertical wine rack right on the wall.

ROOM TO ROOM

OPPOSITE When painting only one room in a saturated shade, you'll always have the challenge of transitioning colors to the next room. Rather than thinking of the rooms in your home as completely separate spaces, you should have them speak to each other in some way. With this dining room next to a deep blue room, it is important to have touches of blue so the rooms relate to each other. Reds, pinks, and tans contrast nicely with and feel as visually exciting as the blue but are also right for the laid-back mood of this room.

A. The runner picks up the blue wall color to help the two rooms relate.

B. Large white flowers contrast against the dark blue walls.

C. Bauhaus-style cantilever chairs look new lined in black that picks up the black in the door.

D. Glasses and a tagine on the table echo the red in this art.

THIS PAGE Mixing woods can feel tricky, but in this sunny breakfast nook, all of these woods tell a coherent story, which even travels to the nearby wall: under the window, a sculptural piece of wall art balances out the folk art on the table.

WHO'S HUNGRY?

I'm a collector and displayer of pretty objects, which is why even in my very own kitchen such things are out in the open, so I can admire my obsessions. I keep my wooden cutting boards and cooking utensils on the counter, which breaks up the marble backsplash and adds depth to the counters. The vintage stools were reupholstered in a soft gray Sunbrella fabric—when in doubt, go heather gray. We infused the space with a few creative comforts: a simple rug (a must in a space where you stand for long periods), a roman shade to keep the space cool when the sunlight is strong, and a piece of abstract art to help set a mood and inspire me to hang out long enough to cook.

A. This art was the inspiration for the whole color palette.

B. A basket picks up the wood tones in the cutting boards and cabinetry.

C. This rug may not look like it relates to the palette, but it ties in nicely with the art on the right wall. Small vintage throw rugs are easy to find at flea markets and they hide stains easily while adding a lot of personality to the space (and to a photo!).

(A)

photo tip   Jump on any opportunities to style your favorite colors in a photo. Here, I styled mine: A bright pink peony sits on the windowsill, a clear container shows off turquoise dish soap, and a roman shade brings in just enough navy for it to be the foundation color without weighing down the photo.

Modern meets her older Italian lover in an all-white kitchen that brings in just the right amount of vintage-rustic touches. A few copper pots hanging over the stove, Le Creuset kitchenware, and, of course, a bounty of oranges transport you to the romantic countryside of Umbria—no passport necessary.

style a unique, useful kitchen

Not big on cooking? I wasn't either until I tackled my kitchen with a few styling tricks. Once you set up this space to your liking, don't be surprised if you start whipping up homemade soups on weeknights. But it's not enough to have a functional kitchen or just a stylish one—in a space that you use every day, fight to have it both ways. Try these ideas:

- **Enamel cast-iron pots set out on the stove.** Made in almost any color, these pots can sit out all the time and are immediately accessible (they're easy to clean, too!). Le Creuset is the classic name brand, but check out cheaper options at discount stores.
- **Organically shaped pottery for fruit bowls.** Large pieces can hold your farmers' market finds on the countertop, and later turn into serving trays and bowls at dinner. Classic hand-thrown shapes in tonal glazes make your kitchen look cohesive.
- **A patterned rug.** Kilim rugs are easy to clean and add color and a soft layer in front of the sink or stove. For extra padding beneath the rug, check out those gel mats made for long hours in the kitchen.

- **Rustic cutting boards arranged like art.** Whether you hang them on the wall or lean them against the backsplash, a variety of wood cutting boards in natural shapes will come in handy almost every night.
- **Tea towels in your favorite colors.** Tea towels are the new tote bags: you can now find them in almost any color, pattern, or design. Keep them folded over the sink or on the counter so they stay within reach.
- **A freestanding island.** Albeit more of a splurge, a kitchen island can do wonders for a small space where surfaces and storage are usually at a premium. An island on rollers means you can rearrange your workspace to be closer to the sink or fridge when needed and easily set it back at the end of the night.

A PASTORAL PALETTE

This look is country meets modern. The whole family will fit at this table with plenty of chairs to go around and a large bench to squeeze in extra seats. The bench really drives home the rustic look; otherwise the early Americana chairs would make the table look a bit more traditional than this homeowner wants. Don't feel like you have to set the table every time you style your dining room. Sometimes simplicity—in this case a linen runner and a huge natural fiber bowl with a bounty of apples—is all you need to make a statement.

A. The runner matches the blue buffet and relates it to the room.

B. A blanket breaks up the bench's long line, while a fur brings in a little luxe texture.

C. Wheels on the table's legs add both whimsy and functionality.

D. These horizontal stripes nicely "intersect" the long table legs.

E. Antique brass and electric candles add to the agrarian feel of the room.

F. This arrangement imitates the flowers in the art.

COUNTRY COZY

This Spanish-style farmhouse kitchen is testament that blue and black can live very well together. Cool blue cabinets modernize a rustic kitchen, while graphic black-and-cream tile backsplash stays true to the house's Spanish influence. Mimicking the black appliances, the black accents feel right at home and give this Old World style kitchen an edge. White and wood are warm neutrals that weave the black and blue together.

A. Brackets dress up simple white shelves nicely.

B. Open shelving helps the smallish kitchen feel more spacious and open.

C. Two wood cutting boards bridge the sides of the kitchen.

D. A rug adds a few extra colors to keep the room from feeling flat, and red apples pick up on its hues.

E. White dahlias carry your eye from the sink to the roman shade.

OPPOSITE Don't be afraid to hang an oversized piece of art over a buffet—just make sure it's either slightly smaller or bigger than the buffet. The brass helmet adds an edge, while a simple tray grounds the barware and bottles. A black-finished ladderback chair has just enough burnish on its arms and legs to match the brown undertones of the blue buffet.

photo tip (**THIS PAGE**) Rather than organizing a blue pot above a stack of blue plates and white above white, we "crisscrossed" the colors between shelves so that your eye moves diagonally across the photo and not just up and down. The art turns ordinary stacks of plates into a stylish vignette.

THIS PAGE A sweet, traditional breakfast nook feels like something out of a European countryside with the addition of greenery and an antique painting at the left. Outfitted with a crystal chandelier, this space feels celebratory, even though it's a place meant for everyday use. An open window, fresh-cut grapefruit, and a carafe of orange juice make you want to curl up at that table with the morning paper.

OPPOSITE Cool oxfords and a graphic scarf pulled off just inside the home reinforce the black-and-white palette in this kitchen nook, which is right off the entryway. The melon, teapot, and tray pull the colors of the painting onto the table, and tell the story of what possibilities can happen in this dining table.

delicious decor

If you love to entertain, then you should invest in a few luxuries so that guests feel comfortable and relaxed during your long conversations over dinner. Make sure your furniture and accessories reinforce the feeling:

- Upholstered chairs make sitting for long periods an indulgence, and they instantly dress up the space. If you don't have any, then make sure to move the party to your living room for after-dinner drinks, especially if anyone starts shifting in his or her seat.

- Go all out with a dramatic centerpiece—but keep it low. Don't spend tons of money on a floral arrangement that you have to move out of the way in order to see your guests (that's assuming you want to see your guests).

- Have fun with your glassware. It doesn't matter what drink goes in what glass, as long as there are ample drinks for all. Break out a decorative glass, and everyone will feel so glamorous holding it that they won't judge a thing.

- Mix in a bench to keep your table from looking too chair-heavy. It'll also help a gussied-up space feel a bit more masculine and balanced.

- Candles make everyone look beautiful. If you can't dim your lights, try turning them off and lighting a corner with a small lamp. Then let the table candlelight cast a glow.

- A tonal color palette will reinforce a relaxing atmosphere. Go with more serious colors in your napkins and table runner, like gray or blue, and see how they transform the room. For dinnerware, white is always best, as it lets the food you worked so hard to prepare (or have catered!) shine.

07

bedrooms

Who needs to run to the store when this space might already have all the fun styling tools you want to play with? Perfume bottles, mirrors, heels, throws—look around your bedroom and bathroom and pull it all together in pretty vignettes that grace your dresser top, nightstand, bed—even that lonely corner near the closet. Get personal, too, as this space doesn't need to be seen by others. Goofy photos that make you laugh, a cracked teapot you can't part with but are too embarrassed to use . . . we'll just keep it all between the two of us.

TRANQUIL TONES

I can get sophisticated if I want to, see? A toned-down color palette relaxes this traditional bedroom with its tufted bed, black window moldings, and antique Provençal nightstands. To give it a lush look, we channeled our inner princess as we dressed the bed with four euros, two king shams, two standards, and throw pillows. Not many folks want to sleep in a uber-formal bedroom, so a few touches add an everyday vibe: a duvet with a little wrinkle, a casually folded bed throw, a sisal rug, and simple curtains that are pushed open rather than tied back. It's a look that totally puts you to sleep—in the very best way.

A. Vintage theater seats create an unexpected end-of-bed bench.

B. Sisal is a calming (and inexpensive) option for a huge rug in the bedroom.

C. Matching nightstands and bedside lamps reinforce the bed's traditional look.

PRIZE
STORIES   THE O.HENRY AWARDS

HOW TO BE LOST

Outliers   MALCOLM
                  GLADWELL

PLAY IT AS IT LAYS

A TICKET
TO RIDE

INVISIBLE MAN

OPPOSITE It never hurts to use books in your color palette, especially when styling a formal room. Serving as a pedestal, they also help bump up the scale of this tiny lamp.

‹ **why this works**

With all of the light tones in this bedroom, it would be tempting to go full-on princess dresser here. But we needed to add some "dude" so both parties feel represented. Here are a few ways we kept this style loose and laid-back:

- This feminine dresser takes on a farmhouse masculine vibe with a dark distressed finish (just think how saccharine it might seem in white).

- We skipped the frames and just leaned a fun photo booth strip against the mirror.

- A tray in a contrasting finish catches your attention for a dresser-top vignette.

- The flowers keep the whole thing from looking too dark and handsome.

SUBTLE STYLE

OPPOSITE Hidden storage with a built-in headboard? Yes, please. This room solves the little square footage problem without skimping on style. With an arched headboard—encased in woodwork and dressed in tufted fabric—this room is totally feminine, regal, and sophisticated. To expand the space even more we dressed the bed with a tonal mix of cotton, mohair, linen, and quilted fabric, skipping any busy patterns. Tip: In small spaces resist the urge for large-scale, strong prints. They'll only stop your eye and make the space feel small. The visual chaos they create can be exciting in the right space, but claustrophobic in some bedrooms.

A. A plant peeking out adds energy to the soft, quiet textures.

B. Tonal bedding with subtle patterns keeps the space calm so it looks bigger.

C. White built-ins keep clutter tucked away so the focus stays on the feature bed.

D. Pale aubergine (not just purple, mind you) is a great color for a tonal room as it works just like a neutral.

THIS PAGE We styled two euros, two standards, and three decorative pillows—all different sizes, colors, and textures but in the same soft color palette.

SWEET SLUMBER

My first instinct in this space was to go wild with color and make it exciting to stay in. Then I stepped back after a crazy multi-colored paint job and realized that it wasn't working. What was I thinking? Luckily, paint is an easy risk to take and also to fix and so I repainted the room in Old Faithful by Dutch Boy. Now I get lots of oohs and ahhs (and, ahem, unexpected self-invitations) when friends walk into our guest room because it's so calming to set foot in. Decorating a guest room is a great excuse to pull out all of your styling stops— especially if those objects can make a weekend guest feel more at home. What surprised me when I styled this space is that rather than adding on a retreat just for guests, I gained a room that I also use for myself, as now I spend more time in it than before.

A. We bumped up the contrast on the pillows and the end-of-bed bench so this quiet room had enough style without feeling overpowering.

B. Art in guest rooms should be crowd-pleasers but still interesting. Skip the cheesy landscapes; go for the cool, unexpected pieces.

C. A tucked-in bed looks hotel-like and makes guests feel like you've been awaiting their stay (even if you just finished the laundry).

THIS PAGE Let's be honest: no one's getting comfortable in this chair, but with other seating options nearby, it becomes a super-cool sculpture that adds a global style contrast to the room's more streamlined look.

OPPOSITE Don't assume that your guests can take the whole weekend off. They might feel more relaxed if they can steal away to solve work problems quickly in a space that feels fashionable. And who knows? Your styling might actually inspire some of their greatest work.

dressing up the bedroom: 4 fun vignettes

Your dresser and nightstand are two of the main surfaces in your bedroom and, if you're anywhere near as busy as I am, they're probably not getting the attention they deserve. Next to making your bed, organizing them will bring instant style to your sleeping quarters and hopefully these four vignettes will give you new ideas for doing so:

1 Flaunt It If You Got It

Your best style secret is hiding right in that jewelry box. That's right, pull out those rings and pearls and place them in bowls or on a small tray on your nightstand. Of course, a jewelry display isn't complete without a bunch of beautiful blooms—indulge in the nicest variety at the market. Orchids will always look rich.

2 Try a Novel Idea

I always leave out a few of my latest reads on the nightstand. It's a little trick that has a soothing effect and it will make you feel good about skipping brunch and staying in bed on a Saturday to catch up on "me-time."

3 Use Your Street Smarts

Your kid's dresser deserves attention, too. Look around his or her bedroom for styling essentials. A simple stack of children's books, topped with a favorite car toy, puts playtime right within reach. Framed family photo strips are a sweet reminder of your love.

4 Surround Yourself with Inspiration

Let your nightstand hold only your most prized possessions—a marble box for your watch and rings, a few photos from your recent travels, and a bubble vase of farmers' market flowers. I promise that you'll wake up in a very good mood.

LOFTED LIVING

OPPOSITE A small lofted bedroom gets cozy in layers of blue and lots of warm brick and woodwork. This little room maximizes its space without filling every nook and cranny. Two mounted sconces leave room on small nightstands for a few favorite books and a simple vase of flowers. Art books stashed beneath the bed stay out of the way while still (kind of) on display. A map of the east Mediterranean hangs on the headboard to remind the homeowner of past travels. The bottom line? You'll never regret living only with the things you love in a small room. Any excess will just make you crazy.

A. A leggy nightstand matches the height of the boosted-up bed.

B. A vertical art piece helps mask the sconce cord.

C. The quirky and cool trapezoid shape updates this antique frame.

D. The throw and pillows pick up on the colors in the map.

THIS PAGE Pull in one of your favorite collections from another room. Here, a bunch of blue glass fits the color scheme. Consider what similar objects you might have en masse that might fit in the bedroom, whether cute Japanese teacups, decorative ceramic bowls, or metal typography letters.

master
your bath

Whether your bathroom is connected to your bedroom or shared with a roommate down the hall, setting up this space to feel like a spa will do wonders for your day. Try some of these styling tricks—no installation needed:

- **Add an extra seat.** In a room of marble, tile, or other hard surfaces, having something soft will instantly put your mind (and body!) at ease. Try an ottoman or small stool upholstered in outdoor fabric (to counter any dampness).
- **Set out a robe and slippers.** Something soft to slip into after a bath might be the best luxury at the end of a long day. Go for a slim and slinky style over plush and puffy to keep your space looking luxurious.
- **Invest in fluffy white towels.** White will remind you of a hotel hideaway and will help reinforce the idea of getting away from it all. For a special touch, get them monogrammed with your initials.

- **Bring in sweet-smelling flowers.** While I always avoid jasmine or lilies by the bed or in the dining room, where the smell can interfere with sleep and supper, the bathroom is the perfect place for natural aromatherapy.
- **Bring in wooden accessories.** Bamboo or other natural woods add a quiet texture to a bathroom that suggests the outdoors. For a more modern bath, try slate or stone accessories to match marble sinks or showers.
- **Paint your space in a spa-like shade.** White tile and white ceilings call for ice blue, cream, or light gray on your walls—tonal colors used at some of the best spas that relax and rejuvenate. With the lights turned off and candles lit, the walls will blend into the floors and ceiling and the whole room will feel like a quiet cocoon.

FOREST FANTASY

An antique theater screen featuring a forest sets the scene for this bedroom, which is a sight for the senses. Soft textures, rich colors, and metallic finishes are scattered throughout, giving this elegant bedroom a dreamy feel.

A. A deep forest scene sets the tone for the room.

B. Hanging bedside pendants mimic the lines of the trees in the panels.

C. Gold finishes that catch your eye lighten the room's look.

D. A colorful throw is styled slightly off-center so it doesn't dominate the room.

E. A fur pillow connects the rug to the bed.

F. Olive curtains echo the deep colors of the wallpaper.

WINTER WONDERLAND

A white bed creates the ultimate retreat, but don't just stop at the bed. This bedroom goes even further with layers of white everywhere you look: on the curtains, floor, and walls. The details are simple and functional—in a space where you sleep, less is always more. By keeping the color palette and textures quiet, the statement headboard really shines and anchors the whole room.

A. Using a hanging sconce instead of a lamp frees up a small nightstand.

B. An eighties-style brass headboard works because of the simplicity of the tubes.

C. A bright blue pair of heels fills the corner in a fun way.

D. Polka dots add some whimsy and personality to a serious white bed.

E. The shade is drawn just high enough to "frame" the painting.

F. The bedside vignette follows the rule of threes: vertical (the flowers), horizontal (the dish), and sculptural (the candle) to bridge the two.

OPPOSITE A wood dresser calls for getting back to basics with a collection of natural materials. Perfect for a quiet bedroom, these objects are all texture without too much color: rock, gold, and raw rope fibers. By the way, macramé is totally in (better call your aunt and ask to borrow that piece she crafted in the seventies that's sitting in the attic).

THIS PAGE When it comes to lightweight objects such as these feathers, don't be afraid to just tack them on the wall as art, creating a small vignette like this one here with the painting.

photo tip **(THIS PAGE)** Prop
something realistic at the bottom of your
perfectly made bed—in this case,
I casually tossed in a pair of worn jeans,
because who puts all their clothes away
anyway? Since the jeans aren't the focus
of this photograph, you almost miss that
detail, but sometimes the best props just
help set the scene rather than tell the
whole story.

OPPOSITE A built-in nightstand
is a great way to stash your stuff
while giving you plenty of surface for
interesting displays. With smartphones,
there's no *real* need for digital alarm
clocks, so why not treat yourself to a
vintage timepiece instead?

OPPOSITE Classic Americana details like a plaid rug and a cabin-style wool throw loosen up the traditional tufting on the headboard, and the mid-century-style nightstand. Two bedfellow colors, blue and gold, are styled opposite each other (in the lampshade and the throw pillow) to help hold this neutral story together.

THIS PAGE If only every bedroom had a little coffee nook. Most people don't think of putting a table and chairs in a bedroom, but this set-up can act as a private office and a secluded morning spot.

RUSTIC ROMANCE

Layering a bedroom in shades of brown and tan might not be your first instinct, but with a huge window that adds lots of sunlight, the tones feel pure and soothing. Here, a wide range of textures work together: Leather, wood, jute, and wool all emphasize the rustic style.

A. This leather bench matches the headboard and acts like a functional footboard.

B. Burlap curtains and a burlap pillow give the room an unexpected texture.

C. The bed's matelassé quilt adds a pattern without busyness.

D. A wall-mounted nightstand allows for a magazine rack below.

E. The roughed-up kilim rug replicates the artwork on the wall.

PRETTY IN PINK

OPPOSITE Give a gal all the shades of pink she deserves in a bedroom she can call her own. A girl's bedroom is hard to style so that she won't quickly grow out of it, but a white canopy bed is easy to update whenever she wants. For the time being, we took to the posts with a funky felt banner and a plug-in lamp cord that hangs overhead. A sheepskin rug and a bay window bench provide soft seats for play dates and marathon *Harry Potter* nights.

A. Go for handmade dolls from a local market or Etsy, which are much more charming than plastic ones.

B. Impress your kid by wrapping her bed post with a pendant cord and a bare lightbulb—it's so cool that she won't even miss the expensive shade.

C. Give her a pretty throw and a soft rug—a little motivation to make her bed and pick up her space.

THIS PAGE Why worry about filling every picture frame? Leave it empty to tone down the contrast in a bedroom for a calmer mood. This antique frame is artwork enough to break up the expanse above the bed.

pattern play

Mixing patterns might be one of the most overwhelming styling principles, and if you're not careful, it can quickly go wrong. Keep in mind these four easy tips to coordinate an effortless, layered look with different prints:

- **Stick to a strict color palette.** Limit the colors of your patterns to just three or four: a main color, an accent color, and one or two "hits" of smaller colors.

- **Combine different pattern scales.** Avoid styling more than one kind of pattern scale—for instance two oversized stripes—simply because your eye won't be able to tell the difference. To keep prints from competing with each other, go for one large pattern, one medium scale pattern, and one small, "bitsy" pattern. Don't know the difference? Squint. If the patterns look similar, then they're the same scale.

- **Limit your patterns.** Pull out the excess patterns that you're not wedded to and add a few solids to let your eye rest. As a general rule, you should have two or three patterns on your bed or sofa—three to five in the whole room. Make sure to add textures, too, which add depth without vying for your attention.

NEW NOMAD

OPPOSITE Doesn't this bedroom make you want to pack that trunk and take off for someplace foreign? Bohemian details balance the masculine details like the nail studs and a square pillow. A cream fringed sheet, a kilim draped over the headboard, and turquoise and navy glass soften the look just enough. This bed also shows off my best bed styling trick: You don't always have to lean bed pillows against the wall. Instead, layer two flat standard or queen pillows on top of each other with throw pillows facing out.

A. A antique kilim on this headboard adds pattern—plus, it looks cool. (Make sure to bring it to the dry cleaner!)

B. This light wood in the trunk perfectly balances the headboard.

C. A tray makes these three items feel like one so they don't crowd the trunk.

D. We peppered the bed's blues around the room to make the palette intentional.

THIS PAGE A chair, side table, and art create a quiet reading nook with a throw waiting for you to snuggle in. The pink flowers intersect the vertical line of the lamp, while the basket at right draws your eye quietly, adding texture and depth.

THIS PAGE This corner vignette pairs wildly different styles, but it works because the shapes are so similar. The traditional chair matches the curves of a Noguchi lamp and the basket, and each feels delicate in its own way.

ALL-AMERICAN MODERN

OPPOSITE Who says red, white, and blue can't work year-round? This bedroom shows how a few accents can keep you from thinking Fourth of July and instead suggest an updated country cottage look.

A. Gold offers a modern highlight in a classic color palette.

B. A carafe of water is the best bedside accessory.

C. Large patterns mix well with a tiny print.

D. A gray blanket throws off the patriotic palette just enough.

E. The stripes on the rug are positioned to lead your eye to the nightstand.

F. A single large bowl grounds the book vignettes above.

THE STYLIST'S
NOTEBOOK

After twelve years of styling interiors, I have some secrets. I've been around. I've had regrets, certainly, and I can't seem to keep myself away from certain people, paint colors, and stores. It's an affair that is one-sided but is passionate nonetheless. So here are my secret resources, my "go-to's," and my "no-fails." Tell no one.

PAINT COLORS

Choosing the right color for a wall feels like choosing the name of your firstborn—there are so many options out there, and once you start comparing them, it feels like you are going to ruin everything if you choose wrong. I've probably painted sixty rooms, many of which I've loved, some that I've regretted. So at this point I have a lot of swatches that are tried-and-true. Whether you're looking for something happy and bright or quiet and calming, check out these paints that I use again and again. And again.

COLORS

HAGUE BLUE BY FARROW & BALL
My favorite navy—with just enough green tones, it's a fresh take on a classic hue.

OLD FAITHFUL BY DUTCH BOY
A happy baby blue with just enough gray to keep a room calm.

TERESA'S GREEN BY FARROW & BALL
A modern, muted mint that works well in rooms that get lots of sun.

CORAL ECHO BY DUTCH BOY
A light pink so sweet you'll want to devour it in one bite.

FOUR-LEAF CLOVER BY VALSPAR
Bright, rich, and super saturated, this is by far the perfect kelly green.

VINTAGE CHARM BY BENJAMIN MOORE
Purples are hard, but this one is warm and sophisticated (not at all like an eighties dorm room!).

MOROCCAN RED BY BENJAMIN MOORE
When you want to go red (and if you do, good for you!), you'll love this bold hue that packs a serious punch.

RAZZLE DAZZLE BY BENJAMIN MOORE
A carefree color that's great for small accents, like the edges of bookshelves.

TOTALLY TEAL BY SHERWIN-WILLIAMS
A dramatic idea for spaces where you entertain friends, like the dining room.

HALE NAVY BY BENJAMIN MOORE
An intense blue that can go almost black; perfect for the wall that holds the TV.

HOT LIPS BY BENJAMIN MOORE
Often hot pinks go really cheesy—too purple or too young. This one is a keeper—it's vibrant and grown-up.

LAPIS ENAMEL BY DUTCH BOY
A saturated, intense dark blue that hits you right in the face in a good way.

LIMON BY BENJAMIN MOORE
Yellows can often go too "school bus," but this yellow is bright with enough acidity to keep it modern and fresh.

NEUTRALS

OYSTERSHELL BY BENJAMIN MOORE
Great for offices and bedrooms, this is a light gray with tones of blue and green.

GRAY OWL BY BENJAMIN MOORE

A warmer gray—in certain lights, it almost looks taupe.

PORTLAND GRAY BY BENJAMIN MOORE

A pretty and warm gray with a little red in it to make it a tad mauve.

TIMBER WOLF BY BENJAMIN MOORE

A cool, classic gray that's dark with lots of drama.

SILVERMIST BY SHERWIN-WILLIAMS

A muted, French country gray-green that goes great with lots of white.

LAMP ROOM GRAY BY FARROW & BALL

A sophisticated, moody gray—think menswear-inspired style.

WHITE DOVE BY BENJAMIN MOORE

An easy white that's warm without looking beige.

DECORATORS WHITE BY BENJAMIN MOORE

A classic white—one that so many decorators turn to—that looks really white but still has depth.

SWISS COFFEE BY BENJAMIN MOORE

Because this beige has a tinge of yellow, avoid it with crisp-white upholstery or wood (think older homes with patina woods).

SUPER WHITE BY BENJAMIN MOORE

Bright and clean with no other tones, this white doesn't pretend to be anything else.

HALF MOON CREST BY BENJAMIN MOORE

This is the perfect medium gray that is neither brown nor blue. I've had it now on three walls and loved it every time.

SLEIGH BELLS BY BENJAMIN MOORE

When you want a light gray that disappears and lets your furniture pop, this is a good one.

FLEA MARKET FUN

The best deals (and decorating stories) you'll ever find will be at the flea market. But before you go, arm yourself with these tips:

- **Make a list.** You think you'll remember, but you won't. Write it down (with measurements if you need them).
- **Go early.** I'd say that 75 percent of the best steals is snatched up in the first two hours.
- **Look for big first, then small.** I go around once for big pieces that catch my eye because that is what flies out of there first. Then I go around for all the smalls: lighting, vases, accessories, etc.
- **Love the shape (not necessarily the color).** Don't buy something *just* because of its color. Love that shape first—you can always change the finish.
- **Don't be a hoarder.** If you don't need it and don't love it, don't buy it.
- **Calculate additional costs.** Account for all the money you'll end up putting into your find: transport to and from an upholsterer, recovering, and repainting. Be sure that you can afford to invest in larger furniture before you purchase it.
- **Avoid the new stuff.** I don't know why it's there and I don't appreciate it. Skip the new booths— they're a distraction.
- **Dig deep.** If you spot a good vase at a booth, chances are that the rest of the vendor's things are good. Go into the booth to find out for yourself— that's where the real treasures are found.
- **Bring cash and checks.** Cash will always get you the best price. But most vendors take checks. Don't count on them taking credit cards.
- **Haggle nicely.** Dealers love their pieces and don't want rude people to own them. If you are apt to haggle, be respectful and polite.
- **Check the quality.** If it's expensive, make sure it's a quality piece. A lot of labels are inside drawers or underneath the seats. But if a piece isn't labeled, that doesn't mean it's bad quality.
- **Remember: Expensive often equals special.** A rare designer piece may cost a lot, but it'd probably cost much more at a vintage boutique. Sometimes it may seem expensive but it's still a steal comparatively.
- **Pull the trigger.** Every decision is a once-in-a-lifetime opportunity at the flea market. If you pass, you'll never see it again. If you love it, if you have a place for it, and if it works with your current style, then go for it. My worst regrets in life have happened at the flea market.

HIRE VS. DIY

In the process of styling your home, you're probably going to get inspired to tackle a heavy decorating or renovating project. There are some things anyone can do and some things I wouldn't recommend unless you have plenty of time and are willing to fail *a lot* before you succeed. Here is a quick guide:

DIY AWAY

- **Replacing dimmers or upgrading a light switch.** Definitely something you can do yourself— it's just a Google search away.
- **Painting.** Do this yourself if you want to spend the time. If it's just flat prepped walls without a lot of molding or ceiling, then no special skills are needed and any mess-ups are easy to fix. Keep in mind that one room normally takes one day.
- **Laying flooring.** With a few folks to help, you can do this yourself, but the cuts are the trickiest part. If you have a more straight, square room, you have a better chance. As long as you are comfortable with a table saw and are good with measuring then go ahead. Installers charge anywhere from $1.50 to $3 per square foot, depending on experience and how licensed they are.
- **Staining or painting furniture.** Do it yourself, unless it's a serious antique or mid-century gem. Refinishing furniture is just so satisfying; once you try it a few times you'll master it quickly.
- **Painting tile.** You can do it. This is especially successful if you just want a quick update. Don't buy tile with the intent to paint it; painting's a good "we like the shape just not the color" solution.

DEFINITELY HIRE

- **Wallpapering.** It's not worth the risk and headache, so hire this out. I know people who have done this themselves and they have harrowing stories to tell for the first few times. It's hard to succeed—there are patterns that need to be matched, seams that need to be cleaned and if you mess it up, it's *really* difficult to repair. You might actually lose money on the paper itself. Pricing varies on the experience of the installer but I think you can budget $600 to $1,000 a room, and one to two rooms a day depending on how fast he or she is.
- **Lacquering furniture.** Now this is a different beast from painting furniture. For lacquering, the piece has to be sprayed, it needs to be guarded from *all* dust (like in a tented room or booth), and it requires really long drying times. Hiring this out is expensive (a small side table costs around $100; budget $300–$400 for larger pieces), so make sure you really want that high-end lacquer look.

IT'S A TOSS-UP

- **Skim coating your walls (or getting rid of texture).** You can do this yourself but it's *very* laborious and messy and you need many special tools. The process involves a combination of plastering the walls and sanding them over and over again. But I know people who have done it themselves for the first time and it worked well. Hiring someone is expensive (because it's so time consuming); you can figure a room might cost around $1,000.

- **Painting cabinets.** This is not difficult, but it is a commitment. There are a few ways you can hire someone to do this. You can get a painter to spray it (not quite as durable but looks good, takes only two days, and is a cheaper solution), or have someone properly lacquer, which can take four to five days with drying time (estimate between $1,800 to $3,000 for a kitchen). But if you set aside a few weekends, you can do it yourself. Watch tutorials to make sure that you use the right paint. Remember that you often have to paint the inside too, replace hardware (including hinges), and redrill new hardware, and normally that quote above covers those annoyances, too.

- **Replacing light fixtures.** This depends. If it's just swapping in a new fixture in a new-ish house, that is often pretty easy. Watch some tutorials online. At the same time, there have been so many times my electrician has told me that what he thought would be simple turned into something complicated because older houses sometimes have super-weird wiring. You can often find someone on TaskRabbit or Craigslist who can do this for $50 a fixture (for simple flush mount). A proper licensed electrician can get expensive, but you'll know it will get done right.

- **Hanging art.** You can do this yourself, but if you have the resources (aka the dough), then having a handyman or art hanger install everything is a *real* treat because the heavier and more important the art, the more you want to make sure that it doesn't come crashing down.

- **Upholstering furniture.** You can do dining chairs, benches, and stool tops by yourself, but when it comes to anything more major, I'd say hire this out unless you know how to do it and like to take risks. Just like wallpaper, if you do it wrong, then you'll have wasted too much money on the material.

- **Hanging curtains.** You can do it yourself, absolutely, but I often don't because it's just so strangely hard to get them perfect. Hanging curtains so that they just "kiss" the floor isn't rocket science, but it is time consuming and easy to mess up. You need to attach the curtains to the rod and lift it, mark it, and then take it down, take off the curtains, hang the rods, rehang the curtains, blah, blah, blah.

- **Tiling.** You can do it, but I don't, probably because I have little patience for small measurements. Tiling is tricky unless you have a really simple pattern with tile that doesn't need to be cut.

- **Adding baseboard.** If you are comfortable with a table saw, love to measure, and have two weeks to spare, then by all means DIY. My husband, Brian, and his friend have been replacing ours for some time now. It doesn't take a high level of skill necessarily, but is time consuming and can be frustrating if the cuts aren't perfect.

MUST-READS

Inspiration is right at your fingers, and if you ever get stuck, take a break and browse my favorite blogs, magazines, and websites for a creativity boost.

ANTHOLOGY MAGAZINE
anthologymag.com

APARTAMENTO MAGAZINE
apartamentomagazine.com

APARTMENT THERAPY
apartmenttherapy.com

COCO + KELLEY
cocokelley.com

DARLING MAGAZINE
darlingmagazine.org

THE DESIGN CONFIDENTIAL
thedesignconfidential.com

THE DESIGN FILES
thedesignfiles.net

DESIGNLOVEFEST
designlovefest.com

DESIGN MILK
design-milk.com

DESIGN*SPONGE
designsponge.com

DOMINO
domino.com

DWELL MAGAZINE
dwell.com

ELEMENTS OF STYLE
elementsofstyleblog.com

ELLE DECOR MAGAZINE
elledecor.com

EMS DESIGNBLOG
emmas.blogg.se

HGTV MAGAZINE
hgtv.com

HOMMEMAKER
hommemaker.com

HOUSE BEAUTIFUL MAGAZINE
housebeautiful.com

THE HOUSE THAT LARS BUILT
thehousethatlarsbuilt.com

THE INTERIORS ADDICT
theinteriorsaddict.com

THE JEALOUS CURATOR
thejealouscurator.com

JUSTINA BLAKENEY
justinablakeney.com

KINFOLK MAGAZINE
kinfolk.com

LITTLE GREEN NOTEBOOK
littlegreennotebook.blogspot.com

LONNY MAGAZINE
lonny.com

MARTHA STEWART MAGAZINE
marthastewart.com

MRS. LILIEN
blog.mrslilien.com

MY DOMAINE
mydomainehome.com

OH JOY!
ohjoy.com

SFGIRLBYBAY
sfgirlbybay.com

TRADITIONAL HOME MAGAZINE
traditionalhome.com

VINTAGE REVIVALS
vintagerevivals.com

VOGUE LIVING AUSTRALIA
vogue.com.au

YOUNG HOUSE LOVE
younghouselove.com

HOW TO BECOME A STYLIST

"Stylist" is a bit of a buzzword right now. Everyone wants to become one, a lot of people consider themselves one, but few people are actually getting paid to do it enough to call it a career. Coming from the editorial photography world, I have loads of advice for someone aspiring to make a living as a prop stylist.

1 **Live where the work is.** If you are serious about it, move to New York or San Francisco. Sure, you can book jobs here and there if you don't, but you'll never truly reach the success you want if you are not in the city in which the industry thrives. You need to learn from the best in order to have a reference point for even what "the best" means. This isn't meant to sound snobby. The Internet has opened up the world to lifestyle blogs, photography, and styling to everyone—but it's hard to sustain a career solely in the blogosphere. It would be like aspiring to become a fisherman in Nevada. Sure, it could happen but man, just move to Alaska and you could get rich.

2 **Become a freelancer.** If you are looking for more of a casual career as a stylist, then you can do that anywhere. Contact successful local Realtors and offer to stage a home and style their photos for free. Or contact big interior designers and offer them your services. They'll see how valuable you are and you'll get hired. Will this lead to features in *Vogue Living*? Maybe not, but it's still incredibly fun to arrange flowers for a camera and take pretty pictures. You'll also build up a portfolio that will lead to better jobs.

3 **Follow a leader.** If you do decide to move to New York or San Francisco, find a prop stylist you love and beg to shadow her for free. Then make yourself indispensable and she will hire you or recommend you to others. Be positive, resourceful, and willing to do anything. You don't need to try to convince her *every* second about how creative you are; just watch, help, soak it up, give positive feedback, and be willing. Once you have your foot in the door, then you'll meet the best photographers, stylists, art directors, and editors in the world. That is how I did it.

4 **Go rogue.** Prove on social media that you are interesting and worth taking the risk on. This applies to virtually all creative fields right now. You could have no experience, no education, and no references and yet still get hired to style/shoot/create huge (and lucrative) advertising campaigns because of how you present yourself on social media. This is the real wild card of the creative world these days, and for many people it's their best shot. We live in a social media democracy and a lot of random people are winning. It's a game I love to watch. Be interesting, have a point of view, and always be authentic. You may not get hired by a magazine, but you might get hired by Nike or Target.

SHOPPING

Whether waking up at 5 a.m. for Saturday's flea market or wandering in a store on my lunch break, I love any excuse to shop. Check out my go-to resources for filling your rooms with long-lasting finds.

GENERAL DECOR

ALDER & CO
alderandcoshop.com

ANGELA ADAMS
angelaadams.com

ANTHROPOLOGIE
anthropologie.com

BLU DOT FURNITURE
bludot.com

BLUEPRINT
blueprintfurniture.com

BROOK FARM GENERAL STORE
brookfarmgeneralstore.com

CANOE
canoeonline.net

CB2
cb2.com

CRATE AND BARREL
crateandbarrel.com

DERING HALL
deringhall.com

EMPIRIC
empiricstudio.com

HD BUTTERCUP
hdbuttercup.com

HEMINGWAY AND PICKETT
hemingwayandpickett.com

HOUSE & HOLD
houseandhold.com

IKEA
ikea.com

JONATHAN ADLER
jonathanadler.com

THE LAND OF NOD
landofnod.com

LAWSON-FENNING
lawsonfenning.com

LULU & GEORGIA
luluandgeorgia.com

NICKEY KEHOE
nickeykehoe.com

ORGANIC MODERNISM
organicmodernism.com

POKETO
poketo.com

POTTERY BARN
potterybarn.com

ROOM & BOARD
roomandboard.com

SERENA & LILY
serenaandlily.com

TARGET
target.com

WEST ELM
westelm.com

WHITE ON WHITE
whiteonwhite.com

WISTERIA
wisteria.com

YOLK
shopyolk.com

LIGHTING

ALL MODERN
allmodern.com

APPARATUS STUDIO
apparatusstudio.com

BRENDAN RAVENHILL
brendanravenhill.com

CIRCA LIGHTING
circalighting.com

DELIGHTFULL
delightfull.eu

LAMPS.COM
lamps.com

LAMPS PLUS
lampsplus.com

ONE FORTY THREE
shop.onefortythree.com

REJUVENATION
rejuvenation.com

SCHOOLHOUSE ELECTRIC
schoolhouseelectric.com

VISUAL COMFORT
visualcomfortlightinglights.com

RUGS

DASH & ALBERT
dashandalbert.annieselke.com

DWELL STUDIO
dwellstudio.com

HD BUTTERCUP
hdbuttercup.com

JONATHAN ADLER
jonathanadler.com

LOLOI
loloirugs.com

MADELINE WEINRIB
madelineweinrib.com

PLUSH RUGS
plushrugs.com

THE RUG COMPANY therugcompany.com/us	**BECKY COMBER** beckycomber.com	**LIESL PFEFFER** lieslpfeffer.com	**SAATCHI** saatchiart.com
RUGS DIRECT rugs-direct.com	**CASTLE & THINGS** castleandthings.com.au	**LITTLE PAPER PLANES** littlepaperplanes.com	**SOCIETY 6** society6.com
RUGS USA rugsusa.com	**DEBBIE CARLOS** debbiecarlos.com	**MAMMOTH & CO** mammoth.co	**THE TAPPAN COLLECTIVE** thetappancollective.com

ART

20 X 200
20x200.com

ANIMAL PRINT SHOP
theanimalprintshop.com

ART.COM
art.com

ARTFULLY WALLS
artfullywalls.com

ESCUELA DE CEBRAS
sindromedediogenes
.squarespace.com

ETSY
www.etsy.com

HALEY ANN ROBINSON
haleyannrobinson.com

THE JEALOUS CURATOR
thejealouscurator.com

MARCUS WALTERS
marcuswalters.com

MICHELLE ARMAS
michellearmas.com

THE POST FAMILY
thepostfamily.com

PURE PHOTO
purephoto.com

TELLES FINE ART
tellesfineart.com

WALLPAPER

5QM
5qm.de

ABIGAIL EDWARDS WALLPAPER
shop.abigailedwards.com

		TABLETOP	KAUFMANN MERCANTILE

ASTEK WALLCOVERINGS
astekwallcovering.com

MIMOU
mimou.se

TABLETOP

KAUFMANN MERCANTILE
kaufmann-mercantile.com

CAVERN
cavernhome.com

MINAKANI
minakanilab.com

DESIGN WITHIN REACH
dwr.com

LEIF
leifshop.com

FARROW & BALL
http:us.farrow-ball.com

MISSPRINT
missprint.co.uk

ELEPHANT CERAMICS
elephantceramics.com

MARK & GRAHAM
markandgraham.com

FERM LIVING
fermliving.com

OSBORNE & LITTLE
osborneandlittle.com

FISH'S EDDY
fishseddy.com

MUHS HOME
muhshome.com

HYGGE & WEST
hyggeandwest.com

WALL & DECO
wallanddeco.com

HEATH CERAMICS
heathceramics.com

THE NEW STONE AGE
newstoneagela.com

JULIA ROTHMAN
juliarothman.com

WALNUT
walnutwallpaper.com

JOHN DERIAN
johnderian.com

OK
okthestore.com

KREMELIFE
kremelife.com

KATE SPADE SATURDAY
saturday.com

PLASTICA
plasticashop.com

TABLE ART
tableartonline.com

UP IN THE AIR
SOMEWHERE
etsy.com/shop/upinthe
airsomewhere

ZARA HOME
zarahome.com

ZINC DETAILS
zincdetails.com

BEDDING & LINENS

CAITLIN WILSON
caitlinwilsontextiles.com

DWELL STUDIO
dwellstudio.com

GARNET HILL
garnethill.com

HAPPY HABITAT
happyhabitat.net

THE LAND OF NOD
landofnod.com

MANOR
manorfinewares.com

PROUD MARY
proudmary.org

ZARA HOME
zarahome.com

MY L.A. FAVES

45 THREE MODERN
VINTAGE
45threehome.com

A + R
aplusrstore.com

AMSTERDAM MODERN
amsterdammodern.com

BIG DADDY'S
bdantiques.com

COUNTERPOINT
RECORDS & BOOKS
counterpointla.com

GARDE
gardeshop.com

GIBSON
garygibson.com.word
press

HAMMER AND SPEAR
hammerandspear.com

HD BUTTERCUP
hdbuttercup.com

HEATH CERAMICS
heathceramics.com

HEMINGWAY AND
PICKETT
hemingwayandpickett.com

INHERITANCE
inheritanceshop.com

LAWSON-FENNING
lawsonfenning.com

MAISON MIDI
maison-midi.com

MATTERS OF SPACE
mattersofspace.com

MIDCENTURY
midcenturyla.com

MOHAWK GENERAL
STORE
mohawkgeneralstore.com

NICKEY KEHOE
nickeykehoe.com

OK
okthestore.com

POKETO
poketo.com

REFORM SCHOOL
reformschoolrules.com

SAM KAUFMAN
samkaufmangallery
.1stdibs.comsearch.php

SANTIAGOS

SHERMAN OAKS
ANTIQUE MALL
soantiquemall.com

SHOPCLASS
shopclassla.com

SPITFIRE GIRL
spitfiregirl.com

SUNBEAM VINTAGE
sunbeamvintage.com

TORTOISE
turquoise-la.com

WERTZ BROTHERS
wertzbrothers.com

YEAH RENTALS
yeahrentals.com

YOLK
shopyolk.com

ACKNOWLEDGMENTS

Creating this book was a lot like starting a family. I always *knew* that it would be in my future, but I put it off every year. Ironically, I decided it was the right time when I was seven months pregnant. I know, who thinks it's possible to meet deadlines with a newborn?! I'm not a total idiot, though, and I hired the most talented people I knew to help me make the best book possible.

A huge thank-you to the designers and homeowners who welcomed us into their beautifully decorated homes for my book. I'm forever grateful to Mike Andrew, Sally Breer, Tomer Devito, Brian Faherty, Shanna Feste, Jessica Helgerson, Scott Horne, Taylor Jacobson, Emily Katz, Ellen Lacomte, McShane Murnane, David Pierce, Adam Porterfield, Noah Riley, Jason Tauritz, and Corbett Tuck.

To Angelin Borsics, who was my original editor at Potter Style. From the beginning, we had this effortless relationship—so much so that when she left Potter, I hired her as my writer. So thank you, Angelin, for your intelligence, persistence, loveliness, and broad knowledge of design. For the record, I care about *you* a lot, and I hope you feel at least one-tenth as appreciated as you are—because even that would be a lot.

To David Tsay, the master photographer. I've worked with David now for eight years—he is the most excellent interiors photographer in L.A. Thank you so much, David, for being so incredibly lovely to work with, for never being bummed that I wanted to try another angle, for always being on time, for accepting my love of GIFs, and, most important, for producing topnotch, cover-worthy photographs *every single day*.

To Scott Horne, the master stylist. While I could have styled the whole book, I knew that I couldn't be the only eyes on the styling of every single shot over six weeks of shooting. I needed backup and Scott is extremely hardworking, with impeccable and rebellious taste—and just one of my favorite people.

When Aliza Fogelson inherited this book project, I wondered, *Does she get my style and my sense of humor and jokes, which aren't that funny, but I insist on making them anyway?* Well, it turns out that she understood all of those things. I am lucky to have her. She made sure that the book got done in time. She knew when to be delicate and when to be forceful, and did so always with the feeling of warmth. Thanks, Aliza.

Thanks, also, to everyone else who made my book more beautiful than I could have imagined, especially the folks at Potter, including La Tricia Watford, Amy Boorstein, and Luisa Francavilla. Margaret King, my superb agent, thank you for championing my work and guiding me to the best publisher. You rock.

I might have the two greatest people in the world working for me: Ginny Macdonald and Brady Tolbert. While we were shooting, they were holding down the fort, taking care of the studio, blog, and business. And they *always* did it with a smile and a positive attitude.

To Brian and Charlie, my husband and my son. Brian did the most wonderful thing a husband could do while I made this book: he was an extra-amazing dad to Charlie. Brian and I have been together more than 15 years and I knew I could get away with neglecting him for short periods of time without repercussions. But it was Charlie's first year on this earth, and I just couldn't fathom the idea of my little baby not being as happy as he could be. So Brian took over and killed it as a dad, while supporting me emotionally. Meanwhile, Charlie became our figurative "3 o'clock coffee"—just when we were about to fade and get grumpy, he'd pop in and make us all smile.